conran's
BASIC BOOK OF
HOME GARDENING

VIKING

conran's
BASIC BOOK OF
HOME GARDENING

A complete guide
for the first-time gardener

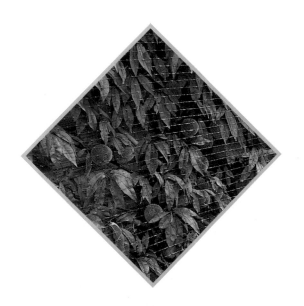

STEFAN BUCZACKI

VIKING

VIKING

Viking Penguin Inc., 40 West 23rd Street,
New York, New York 10010, U.S.A.
Penguin Books Ltd, 27 Wrights Lane, London W8 5TZ
(Publishing & Editorial), and Harmondsworth, Middlesex,
England (Distribution and Warehouse)
Penguin Books Australia Ltd, Ringwood,
Victoria, Australia
Penguin Books Canada Limited, 2801 John Street,
Markham, Ontario, Canada L3R 1B4
Penguin Books (N.Z.) Ltd, 182–190 Wairau Road,
Auckland 10, New Zealand

Text copyright © Stefan Buczacki 1988
Artwork copyright © Conran Octopus Limited 1988

U.S. Consultants Joanna Chisholm, Paul Meyer

First published in 1988 by Viking Penguin Inc.
Published simultaneously in Great Britain

Photograph credits appear on page 192.

Library of Congress Cataloging-in-Publication Data
Buczacki, S. T.
  Conran's basic book of home gardening.

  Includes index.
  1. Gardening. I. Conran's (Firm) II. Title.
SB453.B833 1988   635   87-45958
ISBN 0-670-81773-2

Printed in Hong Kong
by Mandarin Publishers Limited

Contents

Part 1

WHERE TO BEGIN

Gardening is one of the most enjoyable and accessible of the creative arts. It can be at the same time relaxing, therapeutic, rewarding and immensely satisfying or it can be tiresome, exasperating and thoroughly disappointing. So if you have recently acquired a garden and want to get the best out of it, where do you begin?

You can plunge in at the deep end, rush off to the nearest garden supply store, buy a range of tools and plants, rush back to your garden and begin planting. Or you can arm yourself with a small library of gardening books, attend lectures and listen carefully to the advice offered on radio and television programs until you feel you have reached the point where success is assured. I don't believe that either approach is the correct one. By rushing in, you will inevitably make big mistakes and almost certainly waste a great deal of money. By lingering until you feel in command of the subject, you are deluding yourself into thinking that there are absolutely right and wrong ways to perform each and every gardening task; and of course, your garden and its existing plants, be they cultivated or wild, won't wait while you ponder.

This book follows a median path; telling you sufficient to enable you to begin your gardening meaningfully and not too wastefully, but encouraging you also to believe that there is no substitute for experience: your experience. Experts may suggest what to plant and where, but these are only general guidelines and can easily be overthrown by particular local conditions and by existing plants, such as a shady tree. With this in mind, the first thing to do is to go out and look at the site itself.

It is within the ability of every gardener to create a home garden that is both lovely to behold and a pleasure to live with. And it need not be time consuming, expensive or difficult.

Looking at your garden

First, think about the part of the country in which you live and the physical features of the location. Are you in the far north, south, east or west, or somewhere in the middle? Are you in a city or small town, a suburb or an isolated community? Is your garden on a sloping hillside, in a flat valley bottom, close to a major road or surrounded by farmland? Are you likely to be affected by salty winds near the coast, overshadowed by mountains, near to a river or in a forest?

The answers will point to certain limitations that will restrict your gardening activity, and will suggest which plants might flourish in your area, for there are two features of the climate that shape gardens and gardening more than any other. The first is the minimum annual temperature, for it is the lowest temperature at which plants can survive unprotected that defines their hardiness and it is now becoming an accepted practice in the better gardening books to give individual plants a hardiness code which, when read in conjunction with a hardiness map, indicates the part of the country in which each can reliably be expected to survive. Don't be misled into thinking this obscure and academic: newcomers to gardening (and for that matter experienced gardeners as well) make more mistakes and lose more money by buying plants that may have always appealed to them but are unsuited to their winter temperatures than they do in any other way. You can make a dry garden rather wetter but you can't make a cold one warmer.

The wind factor

The second feature that will be of great importance to you is the exposure of your site, a matter that more than anything dictates how windy it is likely to be. Wind is an immensely powerful force but its significance goes beyond the likelihood of your fences being felled or your greenhouse glass smashed. It is a drying force too and can stunt the growth of plant life to a quite astonishing extent. Being surrounded by the high-rise blocks of an inner city may have its drawbacks, but it can compensate in affording your garden permanent storm protection.

In the wild, many plants (and especially many fruit and vegetable crops) will fail miserably in many gardens unless their owners take some measures to lessen the force of the wind, and an early investment in windbreaks of one form or another may save a considerable amount of expense, effort and heartbreak over lost plants at a later stage.

It can take a very minor change to the underlying structure of the site to give a totally different feel to your garden. Changes in level are particularly useful and, in the garden below, a drop in the ground level of little more than two feet has added great interest. Such small changes in level can be introduced artificially into an otherwise flat garden. In the garden on the right, the site, although flat, has been given a three-dimensional feel through the planting of tall shrubs and trees and the use of comparatively tall plants in containers. Arbors are also excellent for added height.

LOOKING AT YOUR GARDEN

Sun and shade

Each type of plant has its own special needs in terms of sun and shade; plant it in the wrong position and it will never thrive. But although you can choose shrubs and, to a lesser extent, perennial border flowers and even a few bedding ornamentals that are tolerant of a fairly high degree of shade, fruit and vegetables are rather different. Almost without exception, these must have sunny positions in order to grow and ripen, so the siting of the fruit and vegetable lots is the aspect over which you will have the least choice.

Your microclimate

The direction in which your garden faces (viewed from the house), the relative amount of shelter that it has and, as already discussed, its overall geographical location all contribute to your garden's microclimate. Whatever the general climate in your area, whether it is rather cold, fairly warm, or a more or less average part of the country, every garden has not only its sunny and shady spots, but its slightly warmer and slightly colder and its slightly wetter and slightly drier ones too. To discover all of these small variations will take you a season or two but the effects can be remarkable. The reason that a particular shrub does not thrive as well as its fellows could be due to no more nor less than its being sheltered from the prevailing rain by a large tree or a fence some distance away. Experts as well as beginners can be surprised at the effect of moving an unhappy plant to a better site within the same garden: it is immensely pleasurable to see a plant that was stunted and miserable suddenly starting to flourish and give of its best.

So it is important to study the significant features of your garden. Once you have at least a rough idea of what you can and cannot grow successfully, you can start to think about yourself and your family.

No garden is ever impossible. The attractive summer house and the striking golden Arbor-vitae (left) make the visitor forget that this garden is at the side of a main railroad track. Small sites present no difficulty either: stepping stones (above) take the eye right through a narrow garden to the promise of something interesting beyond, while the tiny yard (right) has been lovingly clothed with the color of roses and summer bedding plants in a way that totally belies its size.

What you want from your garden

All gardens are different, like their owners. Not everyone wants, needs or expects the same from a site. Do you want a solely ornamental garden or do you want your garden to feed you? Do you hope to grow vegetables and, if so, do you want to grow them to the level at which you become self-sufficient? Do you hope to have fruit and, if so, which are your priorities? None of these questions can be considered in isloation from the equally essential matter of the time you have available.

Gardening should be a pleasure, not a chore. Even gardening fanatics surely do not *want* to spend most of their time weeding, watering, feeding or repairing paths. But how much time can you spare for these basic activities? Will you (like most of us) only be able to spend time in the garden at weekends? Are you actually away from home during the week and unable even to attend to essential watering at the height of summer? Or does your work take you right away from home, out of the country perhaps, for weeks on end?

Only you can answer these questions in detail and then go on to consider which aspects of gardening are likely to prove difficult in your particular situation. The plants most in need of constant care and attention are fast growing annual bedding plants and vegetables that have very busy and productive lives to pass through in the space of a few months. With shallow roots they will cry out for food and water for much of the summer. There are ways in which you can optimize their use of the available water but unless you can attend to them at least twice a week, extensive use of annual bedding plants is likely to prove a disappointment. And unless vegetables can have a regular water supply through the summer, a large vegetable garden is an unrealistic proposition. This does not mean that if you have a demanding career you must give up the idea of savoring your own home-

grown produce: fruit offer a much simpler, less demanding, more rewarding means of supplying at least some of your culinary needs.

Special needs

There are other factors to consider before you begin to map out your garden and start work. Children in a garden can be little angels at one moment and at the next, something else. But they are the gardeners of the next generation and the biggest mistake any parent can make is to exclude them totally from gardening activity, even if they must be steered away from parts of it. The very young have an apparently compulsive urge to uproot whatever you may plant, and there is no better antidote than to provide them with their own small area and their own few plants.

Elderly or infirm gardeners scarcely need to be reminded that it is the jobs necessitating bending that cause the greatest discomfort. A lawn and a few raised beds can make the difference between a garden being an agonizing chore and a joy. Organizations may exist in your city to help disabled gardeners. In some areas, there are groups of voluntary workers who will advise or help to build raised beds or to create other facilities.

The time that you have available will be a major factor in dictating the type of garden that is really practicable. The delightful haven (left) of the bench surrounded by pots of fuchsias could be a weekend welcome for a gardener who is often away from home – the fuchsias in large containers and in partial shade should be capable of lasting well for five days between watering and feeding. The garden above would require more constant attention, however, having much smaller containers in need of daily watering and small, more demanding plants in borders.

Essential tools

We all need some gardening tools, and for once the old adage that it is cheaper to buy the best is not necessarily true. The best quality stainless steel spade, for instance, could cost you five or six times as much as a basic alternative and the advantages, other than for the very serious gardener, do not justify the expenditure. On the other hand, badly made and cheap pruning shears are almost useless and may damage plants.

A spade and fork are essential but unless you have a large garden or plan on a great deal of vegetable growing, the smaller versions, usually called border tools, are adequate at first. You will need a hand trowel and fork for planting and weeding. Here, the cost of the best stainless steel is still within many people's reach. But there are several even smaller and less expensive tools that, once used, will be found indispensable. The widger, a straight metal tool about 6in long with a shallow groove, is splendid for removing small seedlings from their flats or pots, while the V-shaped dandelion digger for uprooting individual weeds from lawns can save you from using excessive amounts of lawn weedkiller.

A scuffle hoe is invaluable for weeding and relatively inexpensive. Rakes are valuable tools too, but if you can afford only one, choose a spring-tined lawn rake which can double up on soil. A lawn edger is extremely useful to keep a neat edge if you have a large lawn, but on a small area you can just about manage with the small spade.

Some manufacturers now offer detachable head cultivators – in effect, you purchase one handle and can then add a range of heads (hoes, rakes and so forth) as and when you need or can afford them. The idea is sound in theory but can be annoying in practice when you need two or more tools to hand at the same time.

A watering can is a basic necessity, but check before buying a large capacity can (the traditional two-gallon pat-

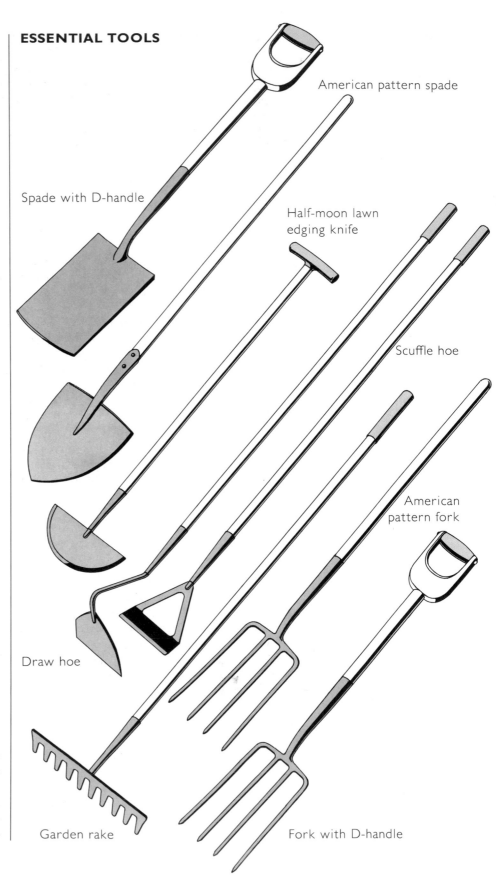

ESSENTIAL TOOLS

American pattern spade

Spade with D-handle

Half-moon lawn edging knife

Scuffle hoe

American pattern fork

Draw hoe

Garden rake

Fork with D-handle

HAND TOOLS

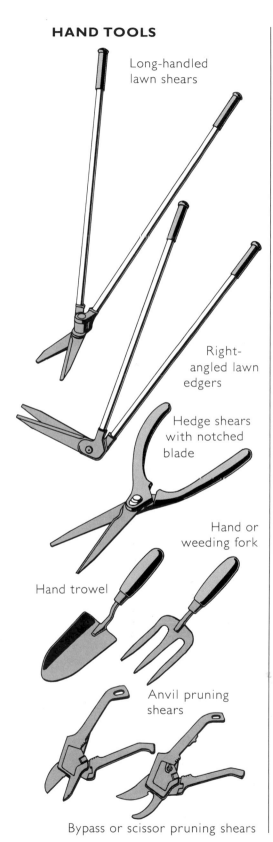

Long-handled
lawn shears

Right-
angled lawn
edgers

Hedge shears
with notched
blade

Hand or
weeding fork

Hand trowel

Anvil pruning
shears

Bypass or scissor pruning shears

tern) that you can lift one of this size with ease when it is full: a smaller one may prove less laborious in practice.

There are two main types of pruning shears. The anvil pattern has one blade cutting onto a flat edge. These are very strong tools and are excellent for cutting hard and old wood, but they can bruise softer stems – like the roses that will be many people's main concern. The alternative is scissor action or bypass pruners which have two blades and are much gentler to plants but are less robust.

Most gardens have at least some lawn and some hedge. A pair of hedge shears will cut the hedge and still, with a great deal of back bending, manage the lawn edge too. If possible buy a notched pair which will enable you to cut through slightly thicker stems, but always handle them thoroughly before buying. Some hedge shears are very heavy, limiting you to about ten minutes' work at a session. In time, and with a bigger lawn, lawn edgers (for the face of the edge) will save both time and effort, but good pairs tend to be expensive and cheap ones are no choice because the handles flex. Later still you might buy long-handled lawn shears (for the flat top of the lawn edge), though these are also expensive.

Machines

After lawnmowers, my next choice for a power tool is a hedge trimmer. Modern ones, especially the more expensive versions with two reciprocating blades, give almost as good a finish as hedge shears and in a fraction of the time. Beware of buying trimmers with very long blades however: it is very easy to disfigure a small hedge with these because of the amount cut in one sweep. A length of about 14in is ideal for most gardens. Some trimmers are rechargeable but this type is inconvenient to use on large hedges as they offer only about 45 minutes of cutting time on each charge.

After the hedge trimmer, I would recommend the long-handled general garden trimmer to anyone with areas of rough grass to deal with. Most of them cut grass with a whirling nylon cord powered by an electric motor. The more powerful machines can be very heavy on the arms, so check whether a supporting sling is provided.

Whenever you are using an electric appliance in the garden ensure that your electricity supply or the appliance itself has a safety cut-out to protect you in the event of the cable being severed. This advice may sound simplistic but the emergency room of any hospital will confirm that a high proportion of accidents take place in the garden, where there are so many pleasant distractions.

Wheelbarrows

There are some tools that seem so commonplace and familiar that no comment on them is necessary. But even the commonplace exist in variety. No sizeable garden, for instance, is complete without a wheelbarrow, but if you have large areas of lawn to mow, it would be worth considering a wheelbarrow that either has high sides or offers the option of an additional high-sided compartment to carry bulky (but relatively lightweight) grass clippings. Another modern wheelbarrow development is the ball wheel pattern, in which the traditional type of wheel is replaced by a large plastic sphere that minimizes the problem of sinking into soft ground.

Whatever tools you choose, it is worth taking some trouble to prolong their lives as much as possible. However tired you may be, resist the temptation to put away any tools without cleaning them. Wipe away soil from spades, forks and cultivators with a cloth and, unless they are of stainless steel, in which case they do not need oiling, wipe them once again with a well-oiled cloth.

Types of soil

No matter how much gardens vary in site, size, geographical location or other respects, they all have one essential ingredient, soil. Many, many types of plant will grow in most soils, but to understand why they thrive in some and just survive in others, it is useful to know a little about the soil itself. Nonetheless, in many ways this is the most variable part of all. A detailed analysis of any particular soil is a specialist task, but there are certain basic soil features of which every gardener should be aware.

Three aspects of your soil above all others will decide which plants will grow in it and the extent to which they will flourish. The first is its overall texture, and the relative amounts that it contains of the four basic ingredients of sand, silt, clay and organic matter or humus. A clay soil can be poorly drained and may even be prone to waterlogging; it will be slow to warm up in the spring but on the other hand it will retain its warmth until well into the fall. A sandy soil, however, will be very free-draining and plants grown in it will often suffer from water shortage; on the credit side, it can be worked and planted early in the season. The ideal soil for gardening is a silt-loam, a soil mid-way between the extremes.

The second fundamental feature of soil is its pH. This is the measurement of how acid or alkaline it is, graded on a scale from 0–14, the lower end being acid and the upper end alkaline. The mid-point of 7 is called neutral. Most plants, certainly most vegetables, prefer a soil slightly on the acid side of neutral and often cannot take up some nutrients satisfactorily if it varies too far from this. Some plants, among them rhododendrons and blueberries, like an acidic soil. You can obtain a rough estimate of your soil's pH with one of the small testing kits that can be bought from large garden supply stores. Most state cooperative agents provide a soil testing service for a modest fee. If the pH is too low (acid), this can be remedied by adding lime – most test kits tell you how much lime to add in response to a particular reading. Alkaline soil is more difficult to change: adding sulfer, aluminum sulfate or ferrous sulfate may help, but this can prove costly on a large area. In general, it is best to select plants that are well adapted to existing soil conditions.

The third and final soil feature is perhaps the most obvious: its depth. There is very little that you can do, of course, to deepen a shallow soil, but you can create some raised beds which will enable you to grow plants that require deeper soil.

SOIL TESTING KIT

I Collect samples of soil from trowel depth, taking five from within each sample area of around one square yard and mix them together.

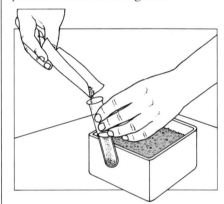

2 Transfer a small subsample into the test tube provided and add the indicator liquid in the volumes that the manufacturers recommend.

SOIL PROFILE

The soil comprises several distinct horizons. At the top is a layer of partly decomposed plant remains or humus. Below this is the topsoil, a blend of more highly decomposed plant remains, mineral particles, air and water; it is in this layer that most root development takes place. Below it is the sub-soil, a region low in oxygen where relatively few roots grow. Further down still is the parent rock or other base material.

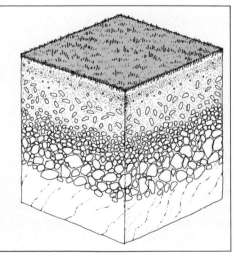

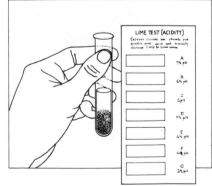

3 Allow the soil in the tube to settle and then, when the liquid clears, compare the color with the chart provided to read the soil pH.

One of the most important of the soil features that govern the likelihood of particular plants succeeding in your garden is its relative acidity or alkalinity. The presence of rhododendrons and also of bracken fern (above) is a sure indicator of an acidic soil, one that will almost certainly need liming before it can be used very successfully for vegetable growing. The second site (left), with vigorous and healthy clematis and honeysuckle, has a naturally alkaline soil – one that can be made more acidic only with great difficulty.

Soil management

Where soil is concerned, there is one golden rule, and this is to treat it with respect; to try to replace with fertilizers the nutrients that plants remove and to try to avoid impairing the crumb structure that is so important in encouraging root growth. Ideally, a handful of soil should feel like and have a crumbly texture which neither runs through your fingers like sand nor clings together in large clumps. You can develop a good crumb structure by adding well-rotted compost or other conditioners such as peat moss to your soil, but the management of soil moisture is equally important.

Soil conditioning, by improving structure, will help the water drain from a clay soil, but on very wet, heavy clay soils, it is worth installing a drainage system. Even in an established garden, the upheaval will bring rich rewards.

Mulching

The retention of water in a freely draining soil is also helped by soil conditioning, but mulching is even more important. A mulch is simply a covering laid over the soil to lessen water loss through evaporation (and it has the incidental advantage of suppressing weed growth). Black plastic sheeting is suitable for the vegetable patches but it is unattractive in the home garden, where you should use organic materials. Well-rotted compost or manure are excellent and easily obtained. Shredded bark makes a good choice, for although it is relatively expensive it gives a most attractive finish to ornamental beds and borders. When introducing new plants, you simply scrape away the bark and replace it when the job is complete. Incidentally only mulch a soil when it is already moist; a mulch on a dry soil will keep it dry. If it is important to apply mulch late in the spring or during a dry spell of weather, it is therefore vital to ensure that the soil has been well watered beforehand.

DRAINAGE

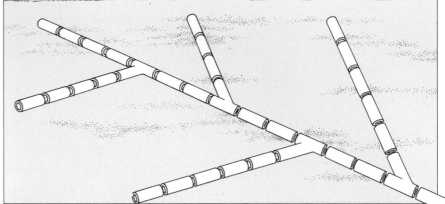

For a simple drainage system, first lay out the pipes roughly in a herringbone pattern and in a manner to cover as much as possible of the area to be drained – space the pipes closer together on a very wet site.

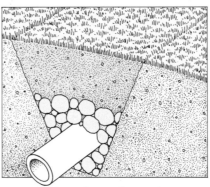

1 Dig V-shaped trenches at least 24in deep, sloping gently towards the position of the French drain. Lay the pipes on coarse gravel and cover them with pebbles and soil.

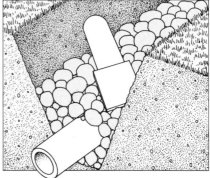

2 Where lines of pipes meet, cut one at an angle of 45 degrees, butt it against a join in the other and cover the junction with a tile.

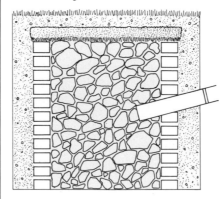

3 Dig a hole of 10 to 15 cubic feet in the lowest part of the garden. Half-fill with broken bricks, then top up with pebbles and soil.

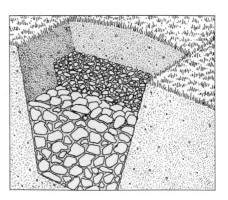

4 An alternative pipeless system is a rubble drain for which you will need wider trenches and large quantities of broken bricks and stones.

If you do not have the energy, money, inclination or need to drain a wet soil, why not create a bog garden and site your garden pool in the center. Bog plants are those many attractive species that revel

in a more or less permanently wet soil, and the two gardens seen here display a small sample of the many delights available. The aptly named candelabra primulas (above) occur in many different colors and shades and make excellent company for large-leaved hostas and water irises (left). The garden here has the attribute of some drier, well-drained soil on a slight rise adjacent to the boggy area. This has afforded the opportunity to plant a small group of the exquisite Japanese maples which display such gorgeous color ranges both in the summer and, of course, in the fall. The fern-leaved Acer palmatum var. dissectum is surely loveliest of all.

Soil conditioning

A soil conditioner is any substance that enhances the crumb structure, and ironically it is the same basic type of substance that improves both a light, free-draining sand and a heavy, water-logged clay. That substance is organic matter, in almost any shape or form. There is a great deal of myth written and spoken about the relative merits of farmyard and stable manure, of garden compost, mushroom compost, hop waste, peat, pulverized bark, chopped up rags and various other organic substances that are available. These materials vary slightly in their plant nutrient value – peat, for instance, contains little nutrients at all while even the best stable manure has relatively little when compared with fertilizers – but as soil conditioners there is almost nothing to choose between them. Nothing, that is, except in respect of cost. For peat and other bagged products can be very expensive while good compost costs almost nothing to make and its production should be an essential feature of every garden.

Compost

The commonly used term compost pile is misleading, for the best compost is almost invariably made not in a pile but in some form of container with free ventilation. The top should be open, although I find it advantageous to cover it at least partially; in the summer, this helps retain moisture while in the winter it keeps out excessive rain. You shouldn't use an impermeable cover like plastic sheet however and the most suitable material is the fairly open weave plastic netting sold as wind-break. One side of the bin should preferably be removable for unloading.

Within the bin, almost any organic matter can be composted, although woody material is only acceptable if it has been well shredded. Annual weeds present no problem but you should always place perennial weeds toward the center of the bin where the tem-peratures will be highest. Diseased matter is acceptable too, with the exception of brassicas affected with clubroot or onions with white rot. You should never add plastic materials, nor such kitchen waste as bones or chicken carcasses which will attract vermin.

It is important to try to obtain a blend of different types of material – not all grass clippings and not all herbaceous plant debris in the same bin for instance. After every 6in or so of organic remains have been added, you must add some form of nitrogen to speed up the work of the decomposition bacteria. Several brands of artificial compost accelerator are readily available in powder form but fresh (not already rotted) stable manure is excellent. It is not necessary to add any more soil than will already be present on roots, nor to add lime, although in dry weather some water may be needed. Compost should be ready in three to four months in summer or about six months in winter.

When used as a soil conditioner, organic matter is best dug into the garden during the autumn so that the winter rains and frosts will break it down and enable it to become well incorporated before the spring. If it is more convenient, compost (and it must be well-rotted so that no weed seeds remain to cause future problems) or other substances can be added in the spring before planting but fresh manures or other undecomposed matter should never be used at this time as they will begin to rot in the soil itself and deplete it of nutrients as the chemical reaction takes place.

Gardeners sometimes tend to forget that soil conditioning is not, unfortunately, a once and for all exercise. All organic matter will break down gradually in the soil by microbial action and disappear. In all gardens, soil conditioning with organic matter should be routine, and the easiest way to do this is by applying a mulch.

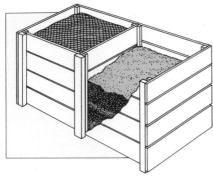

A wooden bin of about 15 cubic feet with slatted sides is ideal for larger gardens. A double structure allows one side to be composting as the other is filled.

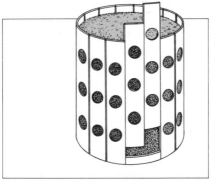

Plastic bins are suitable for smaller gardens, but in all cases, alternate 6in layers of well-mixed debris with fresh manure or a balanced granular fertilizer.

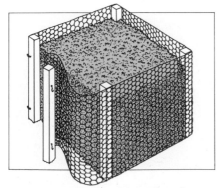

Leaves rot slowly and are best kept separately in a wire-netting leaf mold cage. Add compost accelerator and in about 12 months you will have an excellent mulch.

Every garden soil will benefit from the application of mulch – a surface covering of organic matter. If you spread it on when the soil is moist, it will help to minimize the problems that arise from rapid drying out in the summer. Almost any well-rotted organic matter can be used: compost (above) is probably available in the greatest quantity in most gardens, but the most attractive mulching material is undoubtedly shredded bark, seen here (left) being used very effectively around shrubs.

Cultivation techniques

The two main cultivating tools are the fork and the spade, and each has its own distinct functions. The fork has two main uses; first, it is used for lifting plants from the soil in a manner that offers the least prospect of damage to their roots and without too large a ball of soil adhering to them. It is also used for digging over a soil that is not too heavily compacted; in particular, for the final digging before planting takes place. And by using the back of the fork, you can break down clods to create a crumbly soil in which young plants can readily take root.

The spade is an altogether grosser tool and apart from its obvious value for digging holes, it is used for the first, rough cultivation of well-compacted soil but not for very much actual breaking down of soil clods. Spring-aided spades are now available to facilitate this heaviest of all routine gardening tasks – worth considering if you are among the many gardeners who suffer from back pain.

Even the best soil will gradually become compacted, choking the plants that are trying to grow in it, and an occasional haphazard digging or forking will not maintain it in what gardeners call 'good heart'. Loosely working the soil surface between shrubs or herbaceous perennials with a fork during the summer is of course important, for it breaks through the compaction of the surface layers caused by the beating action of rain and admits air and water. But things are different in the vegetable garden: here you can loosen the soil close to growing plants, but this must be done judiciously if they are not to be disturbed. Use a scuffle hoe along rows of vegetables, to combine weeding with soil aeration, but take care not to sever their shallow roots. Onions unfortunately have roots that are so shallow and so fragile that you damage them if you try to hoe along the rows, so hand weeding with a small fork is an essential task.

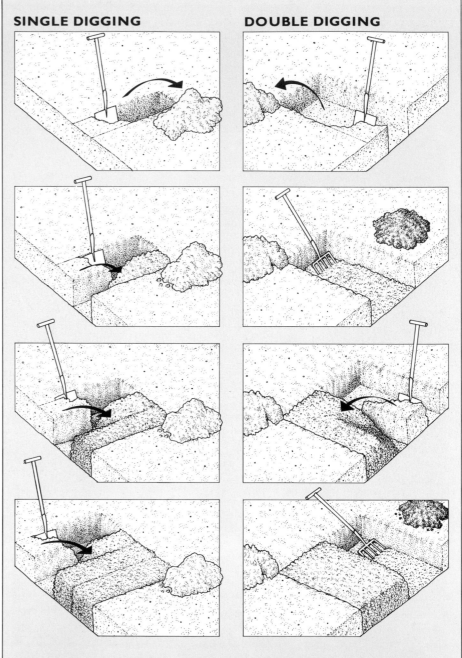

SINGLE DIGGING

DOUBLE DIGGING

Single digging is used for an area of garden, such as the vegetable lot, that is worked at least annually. Work in straight lines across the lot, turning over in front of you a cube of soil of a spade's depth each time. The soil from the first line's digging should be moved to the end to fill in the last trench.

Double dig every few years on the vegetable lot or on any site that will not be dug regularly. Dig to one spade's depth, then fork to a further spade's depth and work organic matter into this lower layer as you do so. Use the soil from the first spade's depth of one trench to cover the lower layer of the previous one.

DEEP BED CULTIVATION

Mark the area for deep beds with pegs and string – about 4 feet wide and as long as you wish. Dig the soil for the bed much as you would double dig any other site, but be generous with your application of organic matter.

Although most essential activities can be performed from either side of a bed, planting or sowing may be difficult. The easiest solution is to work from a plank laid across two bricks, which ensures that the soil isn't compacted.

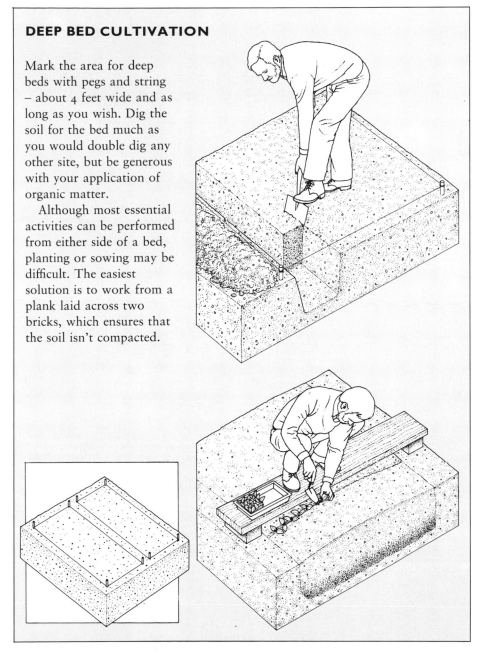

double digging especially, and although you may start out full of enthusiasm for good healthy exercise in the open air, your enjoyment is unlikely to last as long as the digging. Fortunately, there is an alternative to this annual penance.

Deep bed system

The deep bed system has become popular in recent years although it is actually an ancient cultivation method. In its modern form, it depends essentially on performing one deep, double digging and applying plenty of well-rotted manure or compost; after this you don't need to dig again for five or six years. Instead you avoid soil compaction by dividing the vegetable garden into beds within which the plants are grown. Each bed is narrow enough to be reached fairly easily from either side, so you only walk *between* the beds. In practice, it is found that about 4ft is an ideal width although, for planting or sowing, it may be necessary to lay a temporary 'bridge'. This technique has another advantage in that it enables you to grow vegetables at equidistant spacing, rather than in the traditional manner where there are very small distances between the plants but wide gaps between the rows. The row system has been shown experimentally to be an inefficient use of space, and equidistant spacing will give you a better overall yield from almost all vegetables.

The deep bed technique doesn't mean that you will never need to dig again but it should not be necessary to do so more than once every five or six years. Each year, after the old crop is removed, all you need do is to work the soil loosely with the hoe, and fork compost or manure into the surface.

Soil compaction can, of course, occur in ornamental beds and shrubberies, but in this case it results from the beating action of rain and garden sprinkler systems. Here, a thick mulch of organic matter is the best protection.

Single digging

By the end of the season, however dutifully you may have hoed or weeded, the soil between the rows of a traditional vegetable plot will have been well and truly trampled. After a hot summer, it can take on the texture of concrete, but once the crops have been picked or lifted, you will have an opportunity to make amends. One option is to use the same digging system as might be employed when preparing any other area of ground for planting: dig it to one spade's depth in the manner usually called single digging, working in manure or compost as you do so. Then, every few years, double dig to two spades' depth in order to relieve the compaction of the lower layers. This is hard work,

Part 2

PLANNING A FRAMEWORK

Most gardens happen more by accident than by design, and the positions of the various beds, borders, vegetable lots, rock and herb gardens or other features are generally the result of one of two things. They are in their present positions either because a previous owner of the garden happened to have placed them thus; or because the present owner developed the garden piecemeal and placed each feature in whatever space happened to be convenient or vacant at the time. In neither case is the best use necessarily being made of the available area. If you have a totally new plot, there is a clean sheet waiting to be shaped and colored but even if you have a garden that is already more or less established, don't make the basic mistake of believing that none of it can be changed. All or any of it can and should be altered if the garden will then function more efficiently and enjoyably.

Once you have thought hard and carefully about your site along the lines already suggested, you will have a fairly good idea of the features that you want. The vegetable and fruit gardens need sun, but you still have to decide where each of these and the other features should lie in relation to each other, the house, garage, road, drive or other fixtures; either from functional or aesthetic standpoints. This is where garden planning comes in.

Lovely gardens can arise accidentally from fairly indiscriminate planting, though at least a measure of planning will usually give the best results. If you move to an established garden, the challenge is to strike a balance between changing nothing and sweeping away all that is there already. Here, for instance, the gorgeous Voss's laburnum was an existing feature worth retaining, but the surrounding plants were removed and carefully replaced with rhododendrons, azaleas and roses.

Planning the garden

When planning a garden, there are two major considerations. The first is to find a combination of features that functions efficiently; the second is to achieve a balance that looks pleasing. A feature that functions wrongly is a herb garden at the furthest corner from the kitchen; no busy cook will want to walk fifty yards for a sprig of thyme. A feature that functions well is a vegetable garden very close to the kitchen; though it will be visually depressing if, on opening the door, you are confronted with nothing but carrots and pole beans. There is, of course, a compromise option.

No-one, and I mean no-one, manages to design an efficient and attractive garden correctly in one operation. Making small but successful modifications to the plan is one of the pleasures of gardening. As you live with the garden, you will discover, for instance, which little twists and turns of the lawn are inconvenient for the mower and which shrub casts a little more shade than you anticipated.

There is no need to adopt a scorched earth policy if you have an established garden. Draw up an overall plan, by all means, but work through the changes gradually. If you have bought a new house with a building site for a garden, it is a good idea to start by grassing the whole area to keep it weed-free while you relax and plan your ideal garden.

In order to prepare your plan, measure the overall dimensions of the garden and sketch it out, approximately to scale, on a sheet (or preferably, several duplicate sheets) of paper. Then position yourself at the highest vantage point (for most of us, this will be a bedroom window). Note down the tall trees, other buildings and shady spots – and remember that the picture can look very different in the evening from the morning. Then note down the places where the vegetable and fruit gardens could be placed.

If you plan to have a greenhouse,

Simplicity is a virtue in garden planning and it is the hallmark of some of the most striking gardens. The effectiveness of the gravel path (far left), lined with golden foliaged plants and a few unusual flowers such as the round-headed alliums, is immediately apparent and will turn far more heads than many a more complex garden. But it is important to use each feature and type of plant in the most appropriate place. Bold-leaved foliage plants (left) make magnificent additions to a water garden but are right only for a garden with space to accommodate them. This is true also of the island bed, to the right of the water garden, for island beds in small lawns generally serve as little more than annoying inconveniences for the unfortunate mower.

How much better to keep a small lawn, even in a fairly large garden (left), free from the intrusion of tiny islands. The careful placing of an appropriate item of statuary or other ornament is all that is needed as embellishment. The value of a lawn is in offering pleasing color and texture to a large area; to break it up with irrelevant little blobs defeats this objective.

even if not immediately, earmark a place for it at this stage and ensure that another fairly immovable object isn't positioned on the only suitable spot. The one other garden feature that also has rather demanding site requirements is the garden pool, so make due allowance for this too.

Design guidelines

One feature of a good design is to make a garden seem larger than it actually is. Keep the center as open and uncluttered as possible (with a lawn is the most obvious way to do this) and obscure the boundaries. Carefully placed shrubs or climbers can be used to conceal the boundary fences or walls and, if possible, neighboring gardens too. But if your garden adjoins open fields, it is possible by judicious planting to conceal your boundary, making it appear that the garden itself stretches beyond. And curves in beds, borders, lawns and hedges may give a hint of

something lying beyond.

A focal point is also valuable in a garden, taking the eye to an appealing or distant part and away from less attractive or nearby areas. A carefully chosen small tree, a garden seat or even a rose-festooned archway can all serve this purpose.

Added interest and much flexibility in design become available in a garden with changes in level. If you have a site that naturally slopes very steeply, you will undoubtedly consider changes in level a curse. It is undeniably hard work to excavate the terracing that is so essential if the whole of your topsoil isn't to disappear down-slope once you begin to cultivate. But the end result can be visually splendid. On a flat site, it is well worth introducing some change of level to add interest and to offer you retaining walls as additional planting areas. Change the level by excavating a sunken area and spreading the soil removed; not by building a small hill-

ock which will always look peculiar. If you plan to have a sunken area and you can possibly afford the time, effort and expense, the upheaval is much less when done while the garden is new: it may even be possible to persuade the builder to take one additional scoopful with his backhoe.

Once your rough sketches are beginning to show you the overall disposition of garden features, it is time to draw in the more durable components that will link one feature with another – the paths, patios or small yards. It is a useful guiding principle to work outwards from the house. Not all path or paving materials need be very expensive but a good terrace is a sound first investment. Position this carefully – it should, ideally, catch the sun in the morning but be shaded during hot summer afterwards. It should also be a worthwhile size – a table, a few chairs and a sun lounger take up an astonishing amount of ground space.

The integration of hard areas with the remainder of the garden takes careful thought: nothing is worse than a paved patio physically and visually separated from the plants. The use of carefully sited containers can help in softening the hardness (far left) and also in breaking up the sharp lines at the edges. Always remember that any place set aside in the garden for sitting should have sunshine at least for the time of day when you are most likely to use it.

Greenhouses (left) have exacting site requirements – they must be sheltered, yet in full sun, not beneath trees and preferably orientated east-west. For these reasons, it is necessary to be especially careful when choosing and positioning any plants that you might want to use to screen a greenhouse from the rest of the garden.

Creating the framework – shelter

The importance and value to a garden of shelter can hardly be emphasized enough. In most gardens, unless they are very large, the boundary fence, hedge or walls will have the dual function of providing this shelter, together, of course, with marking the limits of your property and affording you privacy. Additional shelter within the garden is rarely needed because a barrier will diminish the force of the wind for a distance on the lee side of about ten to twenty times its height. A six-foot-high boundary therefore will lessen the wind strength for up to forty yards – greater than the width of most gardens. The idea that the more robust

a boundary, the better it will function as shelter is a misconception: in practice, a solid barrier such as a wall creates eddies and turbulence on its lee side, with the result that leaves and other debris from neighboring gardens may actually accumulate in yours. Walls are of course very expensive to construct and most gardeners wanting instant privacy and shelter will opt for a fence. A solid fence creates the same turbulence problems as a solid wall, but it lacks the physical strength to 'stand up for itself'. It has been found in tests, however, that a fifty per cent permeable barrier is actually the most efficient at breaking the strength of the

wind without creating turbulence, so a slatted fence with gaps between the boards that allow half of the wind to pass through will be more effective in offering shelter and less likely to be blown down.

Fences

Fences, of course, have a limited life. Even when you choose posts of good quality lumber, pressure-treated with preservative, they will need replacement; generally after ten to fifteen years. The usual way for fence posts to be installed is with the base set in concrete. This creates difficulties when the time comes for renewal and the

modern square section metal sleeve to fit around the base helps little either – there is still the virtually impossible task of removing rotten wood from within. Given that most six-foot-high fences need some additional bracing, a simpler course of action is actually to use slightly longer than normal posts, ram them into the soil and then brace every alternate one with another stout post at an angle of 45 degrees.

A trellis along the top of a fence, bearing garlands of climbing plants, adds considerably to the aesthetic appeal of a boundary, and can turn a plain fence into a beautiful garden feature. Unfortunately, the plant growth will make the fence top-heavy, especially if the climbers are evergreen, presenting resistance to high winds. This offers an additional reason for supplying firm diagonal braces.

To soften the effect of these supports, you can use treated round 'rustic' poles for your bracing posts, rather than square section sawn lumber. And they themselves can of course be used for the support of climbers. Used in this way, treated hardwood posts should last for at least ten years in most climates. When treating an existing fence with preservative, however, always use a preservative that will be harmless to plants.

A garden boundary that is used to provide shelter and privacy can take many forms. A fence is almost always the cheapest option but it can either be highlighted and made a feature in its own right (top) or carefully screened and used as a support for climbing plants (above and far left). Other, less usual, options include a hedge formed by the old shrub rose, Roseraie de l'Hay (top left), or a wall attractively clothed with large leaved ivy and pyracantha (above left), which require merely the virtue of patience while they establish.

Hedges

1 To give yourself a guide to help you to cut a hedge horizontally, hammer in tall stakes at either end. Stretch string tightly between the two and use a level to adjust it.

2 Take your time when cutting and stand back regularly to examine the work from all angles. A notched pair of hedge shears will cope with fairly thick shoots.

3 If hedges of broad-leaved evergreens are cut with hedge shears, the sliced leaves will turn brown and look unsightly. Hand pruners are better but the work is tedious.

A hedge offers a very appealing alternative both to a fence and a wall, although it has some drawbacks. The major disadvantage is, of course, that it will take time to become established, but you can erect a fence as a short-term measure and then plant a hedge along it, on whichever side is the sunniest. There are other arguments against using hedges; hedging plants are fairly expensive, the upkeep in regular shearing is considerable, and the hedge itself takes up a relatively large ground area and can harbor pest, disease and weed organisms. On the other hand, it can also harbor predators and other beneficial creatures; it provides good stability and wind diminution, and above all, it is an attractive garden feature in its own right.

Hedging plants

There are many possible hedging plants, each with their advantages and drawbacks. Evergreens have the natural advantage of all-year-round appeal. Yew and holly are the best-looking in this group, but are fairly slow growing; *Arbor vitae* grow immeasurably faster, though this, of course, entails more frequent shearing. European beech make an excellent hedge, retaining its brown leaves most attractively through the winter. Privet is rather ordinary but very serviceable. Hawthorn is useful for a quick growing, impenetrable barrier along field boundaries, although it is not, of course, evergreen. Among many attractive hedges are those of roses, firethorn (*Pyracantha*) and barbary (*Berberis*).

Almost all hedges should be sheared at least twice each year (privet is the most demanding, needing at least three cuts to keep it neat). No hedge should be cut between early August and the first hard freeze in most areas. A late summer shearing can cause

resprouting, which is then susceptible to winter damage and can cause the onset of dying back. Flowering hedges, such as roses or hypericum, are best cut once, fairly hard, just after the flowers have faded.

It should be borne in mind that most of these plants are prickly. This is an advantage if you want to keep something out, but thorny twigs can be rather a nuisance. If prickles worry you, then beech may be the best choice.

There is a considerable range of plants suitable for hedges but it is important to try to avoid monotony. An otherwise uninteresting line of hedging can be relieved by careful placing of containers in front (far left), but an arguably better option if you are starting from scratch is to plant a mixture of species. Golden variegated holly, green and copper beeches and yew can all contribute to an appealing patchwork (left). Beech is always an excellent hedging plant, if rather slow to establish. Although deciduous, it retains its dead leaves throughout the winter (above) and thus provides an attractive yet changing screen throughout the year.

Siting and shaping beds

Most of the ornamental plants – and with them the color and excitement – in your garden will be grown in beds and borders. Plan these skilfully; even a small city garden can be transformed from an oblong patch, with everything in full view, to a delightful series of vignettes, with the eye drawn on from one charming scene to another.

Before this planning stage, it helps to get some basic definitions sorted out. I think of a bed as an area of bare soil within which annuals and biennials (so-called bedding plants) are grown, while a border is for non-woody or herbaceous perennials or a mixture of these and shrubs. An area of soil surrounded by lawn is known as an island bed, irrespective of the types of plant grown in it.

Island beds tend to make a small garden look cluttered and cut down appreciably the area of lawn, but they come into their own in a large garden, where they can give impressions of hidden space beyond, in gardens where they are needed to conceal some unattractive feature, or in those closely tended and time-intensive gardens where intricate patterns of bedding plants form the main features.

They should be positioned so that the distance from one bed to another or to the edge of the lawn is in multiples of your mower width; otherwise you will have frustrating odds and ends to mow and will spend time trying to avoid tipping the mower over one edge or the other. It is also good planning to make sure that the curves of any bed or border can easily be cut with either a lawn edging knife or your lawn shears.

There is a place for the straight-edged border but this is usually alongside some other straight-edged feature such as a path. At the side of the lawn, a gentle and simple curve is much easier on the eye. The emphasis should be on simplicity – complex serpentine edgings are labor intensive and tend

SITING AND SHAPING

To mark out an elliptical curve, measure out and mark with pegs the long axis (A-B). Stretch string from A to B and knot each end. Mark the mid point (C) and insert post X at right angles to it, placing X at the desired widest point of the bed. Remove string and fold in two to find the center point. Loop this over X. Stretch the string so the ends come to line A-B. Slip each knotted end over a peg (P and Q). Take a loose peg (R) and, holding the string taut, use this to scratch the shape of an ellipse.

to distract the eye from more important garden features.

Most border perennials have a limited flowering period, and although you can carefully choose a range which will give you continuity of color from spring through until fall, this planning is wasted unless the border is both wide and deep enough to accommodate them; much less than six feet depth is really inadequate and nine feet – if you can spare it – is better. If your garden is narrow you can get round this problem by planting shrubs, which retain their attractiveness for very much longer periods filling in with perennials and bedding plants.

The importance of shaping beds is sometimes not appreciated from ground level – which is why it makes sound sense at the planning stage to sketch the outline from a high vantage point such as a bedroom window. Here the borders have been gently wrapped around a small lawn – the center of the garden is kept open, the rectangular shape is obscured and the boundaries are subtly absorbed into the whole.

Paths and paving

More than any other features, paths can quickly define the shape and proportions of the various parts of your garden. Their basic purpose may be to provide mud-free routes from one area to another, but they also have considerable design value for they can – by being curved or straight and direct – render the overall feel of a garden either hard or soft. If constructional materials are chosen with thought, a path can be a very attractive component of a garden in its own right. There are numerous options, but some are very expensive, both to buy and lay. Perhaps the most costly of those considered here is brick. Bricks can be laid in a variety of attractive designs of which the herringbone is surely the loveliest of all. Choose brick for a city garden or for a country garden where the house too is brick built. It is tempting to use old standard building bricks, especially if you have some left over from another project, but these will crack and crumble quickly after frosts. Hard engineering bricks or purpose-made brick paving sets are much better.

Stone

For a stone-built house, stone slabs will always look right but real Tennessee or other paving stones may be prohibitively expensive. Instead, use one of the excellent modern replicas which are actually much easier to lay, being of uniform thickness.

Concrete

Concrete is relatively inexpensive and quick to lay. Its surface can be enlivened and also made less slippery if you brush it coarsely before it dries. Subtle shades of concrete dyes can also soften its appearance. While it is easy to concrete a path, a large flat expanse for a terrace is difficult for the inexperienced and might be better left to a contractor. Ready mixed concrete seems an attractive option, but the

LAYING PAVING

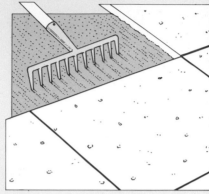

1 Place a layer of builders' sand about 2in deep over a well-firmed base and rake it level.

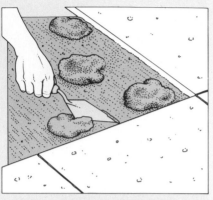

2 Place small mounds of mortar on the sand – one at each corner and one in the center for each slab.

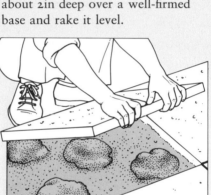

3 Keeping feet together and back straight, lower the slab gently into place.

4 Use a wooden mallet to tamp each slab firmly into place and ensure that it does not rock.

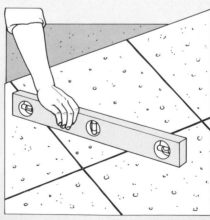

5 Check with a level and if the slabs adjoin your house, ensure that they slope away from it.

6 On a firm site, small slabs or bricks can be laid on sand alone if they have a solid restraining edge.

TYPES OF PAVING

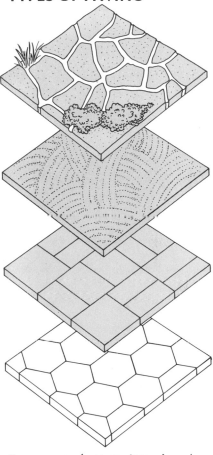

From top to bottom: 'crazy' paving, brushed concrete, stone slabs, and hexagonal slabs – choose whichever is most in keeping with your house.

Paved areas and paths are components of almost every garden and play a large part in dictating the overall shape and feel. A paved area or patio can be unashamedly formal (top) with a rectangular pool or it can be softened in varying ways. Gravel, either alone or used in combination with other paving materials (center), lends a degree of softness, while irregularly shaped stones (left) – either natural or a good artificial reproduction – offer a timeless quality.

minimum quantities available are usually fairly large, and having to lay the mix correctly in the short time before it sets can be a nightmare – especially when it is raining. Hiring a small concrete mixer and preparing batches is a better bet for those of nervous disposition.

Wood

Wood is a less commonly used but attractive path material, most often seen in the form of short lengths of hardwood tree-trunk, set vertically into the ground. It can be extremely slippery when wet, however, so it is unsuitable for a path that will have to carry a great deal of traffic all year round. Much easier to lay and not slippery, but arguably as attractive, is coarsely shredded bark, now becoming widely available. The bark will need to be topped up every season but this can be done at fairly modest cost and a bark path looks delightful in less formal or wooded areas.

Bark chips need confining in some way and the same is true of gravel, but in both cases their very looseness is an advantage, for they can be laid into the most intricate of corners or around the most complex of obstacles. Gravel is also cheap, the very small rounded pea gravel especially so. Maintenance presents no difficulty and comprises regular raking and one or two weed-killer treatments each season.

Cobbles (top) must be set well into concrete if they are not to become dangerously loose. They should also be arranged so that they do not protrude more than about ½in. Gravel (right) is the easiest paving material to lay and seems to flow naturally around bends. Irregularly shaped stone fragments laid in the manner sometimes called 'crazy paving' (far right) are much cheaper than large natural slabs, but patience and good mortaring are needed.

TYPES OF PATH

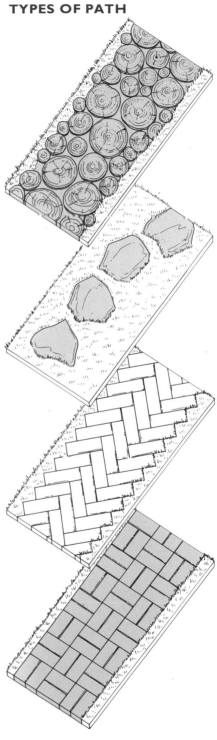

From top to bottom: wooden blocks, stepping stones in grass, herringbone patterned bricks, and basket-weave patterned bricks.

Edgings and raised beds

The firm edging needed to confine loose path materials like bark and gravel can also provide an attractive finish to other types of path. Edgings can be expensive and should be chosen with care. For a small stretch of path close to a house, perhaps between small flower borders or beds, Victorian terracotta edgings in rope-top or similar designs are excellent. It is possible to obtain originals from specialist suppliers or to buy reproductions. They should be rammed in with soil, not mortared.

For large expanses of gravel such as driveways or yards, standard round-top concrete curbs are unobtrusive and effective. But for confining either gravel or bark chip paths, there is nothing as simple to erect, pleasing to the eye or inexpensive as half-round lengths of lumber of the type sold for farm railings. Normally about 12 feet long, they can be cut to length and should be bought de-barked and pressure-treated with preservative. Give each an additional treatment with a water-based wood preservative and secure them, flat face inward, with 18in oak pegs.

But continue a lumber edging upwards for anything from 12in to 36in, use it to enclose a defined area, cover the inside floor with broken bricks or similar rubble for drainage, and then fill the whole with a mixture of soil and peat and you have a raised bed. You can stack half-round timbers to form the edge, but larger planks such as old railroad ties are even better, though they are very heavy and cumbersome to manipulate.

The first advantage of a raised bed is that it can provide an attractive change of level in an otherwise flat garden, especially if it is backed against a garden wall (not against a house wall or you will very effectively bypass your damp proof course). A second use for a raised bed is for disabled or infirm gardeners who have difficulty in stooping. It also

BUILDING A RAISED PEAT GARDEN

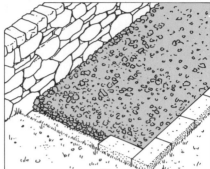

1 It is easiest to build a raised peat garden against a wall or other solid backdrop. Mark the boundary by digging a shallow trench to half the depth of a peat block.

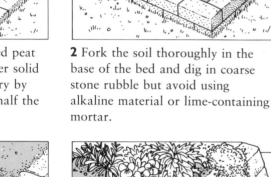

2 Fork the soil thoroughly in the base of the bed and dig in coarse stone rubble but avoid using alkaline material or lime-containing mortar.

3 Build up the bed with a mixture of two-thirds peat and one-third soil (by weight) but don't use soil that contains limestone fragments. Compress the peat gently as you fill.

4 It is easiest to insert small wall plants as the peat bed is being built, as they will then establish better and are less likely to suffer damage to their roots.

EDGING A PATH WITH LUMBER

Hammer in two 18in hardwood pegs at each end of half-round fence nails, placed flat face inward.

Stamp or roll the path and fill with stone chippings, gravel or coarsely shredded bark.

provides a means of growing at least a few deeper rooted plants (including root vegetables) in a garden with very shallow soil. But perhaps the commonest use of the raised bed is to create a small peat garden, an area of acidic soil in an otherwise alkaline region, to provide such delights as summer flowering heaths, dwarf rhododendrons and azaleas or a small camellia.

Raised peat garden

A raised peat garden can be constructed with lumber sides, but it is more appropriately built of blocks of peat itself. You can buy these from most large garden supply stores, then lay the blocks as you would bricks, sloping the walls inwards slightly and inserting small wall plants like ferns between the blocks as you build. Build the walls about 12in high and then very thoroughly loosen the soil inside to a fork's depth. Add peat (bought in bulk) and gradually dig it into the soil. Allow the whole to settle and then top up with peat. You will need to top up again annually. Although the volume of peat needed will be considerable, there is no need to buy the best quality – sedge peat bought in bales will be a sensible option for most gardeners.

For a formal path, and to give a garden a period feel, Victorian terracotta path edgings in rope-top or other patterns (top) are delightful. Reproduction versions are now available.

Raised beds are invaluable not only for peat gardens but also in offering a simple change of garden level or in providing an aid for disabled gardeners. Bricks (left) offer the most permanent edging but durable lumbers (above) are an inexpensive and attractive alternative.

Lawns

Grass is the most adaptable of garden plants and the lawn the most versatile of all garden features. In a large garden (above), use grass to provide a broad walkway between borders, bearing in mind that a very narrow grass path will become a mud-walk if it is used extensively in winter. Use a round lawn in a smaller, square garden (right) to take the emphasis away from its angularity and to help make the area as a whole appear larger.

There is no easier way to maintain a given area of garden in an attractive cared-for state than with a lawn. There are many gardeners, of course, who complain, justifiably, that their lawns never resemble those in seed catalogs. This may be due partly to inadequate or inappropriate lawn care, but in many cases it is because of inadequate or inappropriate preparation.

Preparation

Begin the preparation of the site as long as possible in advance of sowing or sodding. If, as suggested, you are grassing the majority of a new garden to give yourself thinking time, this may seem a contradiction but it is worth taking a little care, especially to remove perennial weeds from any site that will form part of a long-term lawn. My ideal would be to start in the summer by making regular applications of a systemic weedkiller so you should have cleared the area ready for fall sowing of seed.

The essential preparation needed both for sods and seed is the same. After a thorough digging and working in well-rotted compost or fertilizer, you should assess if the site needs leveling. A dead-flat lawn is by no means necessary and a gentle slope can be very attractive but a surface like a switchback will inevitably lead to difficulties as your mower misses the troughs and scalps the peaks. The few hours spent carefully at this stage will be blessed many times in years to come. Before sowing the grass, rake the area thoroughly with the wide spring-tined lawn rake to remove clods and large pebbles. Always rake in alternating directions to avoid renewing the humps and hollows.

The site must then be firmed and I have never found an adequate substitute for a pair (or, better still, several pairs) of feet to do this. It will be necessary to rake again gently during the firming.

SOWING LAWN SEED

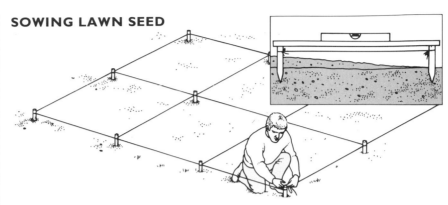

1 To level a bumpy site, mark out a grid pattern of pegs 6 feet apart. Lay a plank across adjacent pairs of pegs in turn and, using a level, hammer the pegs until level.

Tie string between the pegs at the lawn level desired — if you tie the string at the same distance below the top of each peg, you will have a level grid pattern.

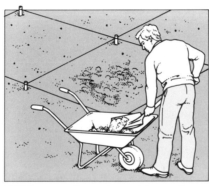

2 Fill up to the string with good quality topsoil. You may need to buy in a load of soil if the site is very irregular but this will be worthwhile in the long run.

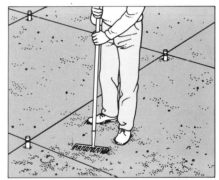

3 Firm the soil as you add it, using the back of a good quality rake. Always leave the surface about $\frac{1}{2}$in higher than you eventually intend, to allow for settlement.

4 Lawn seed should be added at the recommended rate. Most suppliers provide a measure with the pack, a shaker or even a picture showing the density to aim for.

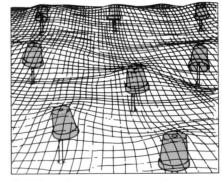

5 Although some grass seed is now treated with a chemical bird repellent, netting provides the best protection. Support fruit net on upturned plastic plant pots.

Seed or sod?

Should you choose sods or seed? Sods gives you a lawn much more quickly but considerably more expensively. You should avoid all cheap sods or any that are branded 'meadow' – this is fine for grazing cattle but not much else. Choose specially grown sods. For seed, choose a mixture containing fine leaf varieties of perennial rye or new, fine leaf varieties of tall fescue or rye grass for a normal, hard-wearing lawn that will be walked or played on, but a fine-leaved blend of Kentucky blue grass if the lawn is more to be looked at than used. Check with local experts for advice on sod varieties best suited to your region.

The importance of choosing a lawn seed mixture with superior varieties of tall fescue or rye grass for an area where children will play cannot be stressed too strongly. And if there is one spot that is likely to be subject to abnormal usage (beneath a climbing frame for instance), it is better to lay sand or an outdoor play mat here.

Mowers

As important as buying seeds or sods and sowing or laying them carefully is equipping yourself with the necessary hardware to convert grass to lawn. For the very essence of a lawn is that regular cutting stimulates the development of what is called tillering – the formation of side shoots from each grass plant that serve to build up and maintain a close sward. Lawnmowers are now available in an extremely wide array of designs and it is worth considering some of their relative merits.

All lawnmowers cut in one of two ways – either by means of a cylindrical arrangement of blades (the actual number depending on the quality and price of the mower) on a spindle parallel with the surface of the lawn, or by some form of rotating cutter on a shaft at right angles to the surface. There is no doubt that the best and most even

SODDING A LAWN

1 Use string and pegs to mark out the boundaries against which the sods should be laid. Open rolls of sod in the shade if you cannot lay them within two days, and keep moist.

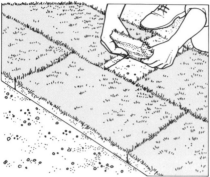

2 Never use small pieces of sod at the ends of rows as they will tear and shrink. Leave gaps within the rows if whole pieces of sod do not fully make up the required length.

3 Fill in between the sods with fine soil. It may be helpful to use a brush over a large area. Never worry about soil spilled on the surface; it will soon be washed in.

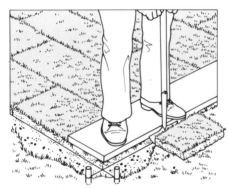

4 Trim the edges by standing on a board and making a cut sloping slightly away from you. Curved edges are harder but lay out a hose and cut close to it.

cut is obtained with the cylinder pattern, and for a lawn comprising a high quality, rye-grass-free mixture, this is a superior choice. The hand propelled cylinder mower is now almost extinct and, for a large lawn, I believe that a gas driven machine with power drive (which means that the engine, not you, takes the weight) has yet to be bettered. If you have a small high quality lawn, an electrically powered cylinder mower is an excellent choice.

But unless you have a large or a particularly high quality lawn, the rotary type of mower is more than

adequate, and for fairly rough grass it is almost obligatory.

If possible, choose a machine with a bagging attachment. It is sometimes said that leaving the grass cuttings on the lawn is advantageous because it supplies a moisture retaining mulch and returns nutrients to the grass. This is true, but if the clippings are especially heavy it is good to have the option of collecting them so that the healthy grass is not smothered under clods of clippings. Also, it is useful for those special occasions when the lawn should be especially neat. When collecting the clippings, compost them and recycle the resulting humus onto your planting beds.

Another useful piece of lawn equipment is the dethatcher, sometimes called a vertical lawnmover. The dethatcher has blades that cut perpendicular to the lawn, thereby removing the dead debris called thatch, which can easily build up in a lawn. Excessive thatch can prevent the penetration of water into the soil and can lead to a buildup of turf-disease organisms. In the home garden dethatching is generally performed once a year, usually in the late summer or early fall, when it is followed by fertilization and an overseeding of any dead areas. Such a time is ideal because it is when grasses are naturally tillering, or producing side shoots, which help thicken the turf after dethatching. It is also the best time of year for overseeding. Since the vertical blades of the dethatcher lightly scarify the soil surface, the lawn can then be reseeded.

A dethatcher is used only occasionally so it is most economical to rent this piece of equipment from your local garden supply store or rental agency. When dethatching, be prepared for a hard day's work since this machine will pull an amazing amount of debris from the lawn. This will have to be gathered and then carted to the compost pile.

The importance of sweeping or raking a heavy fall of leaves from the lawn cannot be overstated, for it isn't simply a cosmetic exercise. Thick layers of leaves will make the lawn surface slippery and will obstruct both light and water reaching the grass. The result, next spring, will be a very patchy lawn indeed. A mulching mower can grind the leaves to a pulp, which will enrich the soil, but even here heavy layers of ground-up leaves should be removed.

For some people, nothing matches the appeal of a lawn cut with a cylinder mower in the English style.

Structural supports

TRELLISES AND PERGOLAS

For full-height trellis, always use strongly made panels, supported on 3in by 3in treated posts. A 6ft post should be sunk at least 2ft.

Lighter weight trellis can be used on fence tops, but when covered in climbers it will all be top-heavy and need additional bracing.

A pergola provides a sheltered area for recreation and also supplies valuable additional support for climbers. It is most easily erected against the side of a building or at an inward corner where two walls join. Always position a pergola where it will receive sun during the part of the day that you are most likely to want to sit outside.

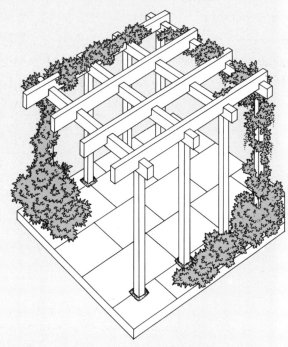

Use halved joints for links between the cross members.

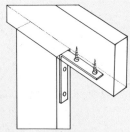

Right-angled metal brackets give extra support.

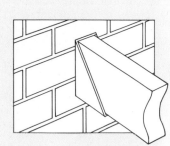

Special brackets can be bought for joining lumber lengths to a wall.

A two-dimensional garden is a boring garden. It is also an inefficient use of space and it denies its owner the opportunity of growing some of the most attractive of all ornamental plants. Provide artificial supports, place climbing plants against them and your garden will be immeasurably enriched.

It is tempting to attach climbers directly to an existing solid structure, but if you provide some means of fitting the shoots a few inches away from the surface, you will permit air to circulate freely beneath and so reduce the problems from mildew or other diseases, and pruning will be simpler. The easiest and commonest way to achieve this is with a more or less rigid, open-structured trellis panel, mounted on wooden battens of about $1\frac{1}{2}$in by $\frac{3}{4}$in. Treat the wood with a non-toxic preservative and use lightweight, diamond-pattern durable cedar wood trellis.

Plastic trellis is rarely as satisfactory; it has an unyielding, unnatural appearance and the white discolors unattractively. For a wall area of more than about 6ft by 6ft or for an irregularly shaped area, use training wire supported either with eye screws or with small metal pegs which can be hammered into mortar and have a hole at one end. The best training wire is coated with green plastic (don't use tying wire as this is thinner and is much too weak).

Trellis can also be freestanding, either on a small scale, as when they are used providing a topping to a fence, or as panels supported between posts. Use heavy duty, square or diamond-pattern trellis in this way to provide a screen for an area such as the vegetable garden, without cutting out all of its sunlight.

More exciting still are ornamental archways and pergolas, used either over a house door or across a path to provide a subtle division between two

parts of the garden. Archways are not easy to build from scratch but it is possible to buy them ready made, usually either incorporating a wooden framework over which trellis is fixed or built of treated rustic poles. The trellis archways are often not sufficiently robust to support for several years the weight of large climbing plants such as roses and it is well worth buying the strongest that you can afford – replacing an archway bearing established climbers is an extremely difficult task. For the same reason, ensure that any wood used for an archway has been well-treated with preservative.

There is scope both for imagination and ingenuity in the arrangement of supports for climbing plants. A lightweight archway festooned with roses (above) is undeniably appealing but is stronger and more durable when made from metal than wood. Upturned hanging baskets mounted on wooden posts (left) provide an original way of allowing honeysuckle or other plants to trail downward.

Greenhouses

A greenhouse is a sizeable investment, but the extra dimension that it gives to your gardening activities and the liberation that it offers the kitchen window sill or the spare bedroom will give you ample rewards.

The ideal position for a greenhouse, though you will probably have to compromise a little, is facing south, with the long axis of the greenhouse running east-west to trap the maximum amount of sunlight. It should be on level ground and away from trees (especially deciduous ones). There are advantages in having the greenhouse fairly close to your house. First because there is less distance to walk in the depths of winter, but also because the closer it is, the easier and cheaper it will be to have the utility service installed if and when you can afford it.

Among the least expensive versions are lean-to structures: these not only save on valuable open space in a small garden but also benefit from the warmth of the wall itself. For a small free-standing structure, I much prefer the traditional span pattern, preferably with a wooden base. The hemispherical or similarly complex designs make more efficient use of the sun's heat, and warm up quickly. Unfortunately, they also cool down very quickly, and they offer a disconcertingly small growing area in relation to their cost.

Most modern greenhouses are made from aluminum, although a few manufacturers still offer the more traditional wood. Wood retains heat better, 'gives' more and is generally less prone to be damaged in strong winds; and, in older gardens with older houses, it also looks better. On the other hand, it requires more maintenance: durable western red cedar is the best material but even this should be treated with a non-toxic preservative every two years. Inevitably most gardeners will choose aluminum for reasons of availability, cost and ease of erection, but it is essential to buy from an established

GREENHOUSES

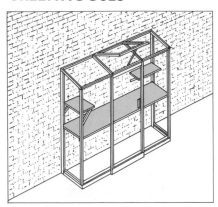

For a small garden, an aluminum miniature greenhouse offers useful growing space against a warm wall.

A span house with wooden base is convenient to use, but like all designs it must have several vents.

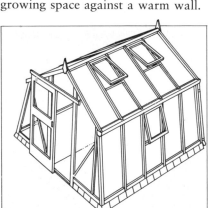

The glass-to-ground house is useful for starting annuals but has wasted ground area at the bases of the sides.

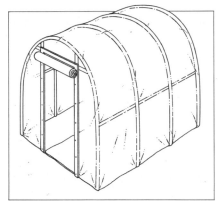

The plastic house with a metal frame is scarcely lovely but offers low-cost protected growing space.

COLD FRAMES

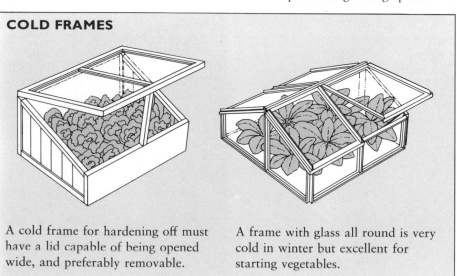

A cold frame for hardening off must have a lid capable of being opened wide, and preferably removable.

A frame with glass all round is very cold in winter but excellent for starting vegetables.

and reputable manufacturer. Poorly built aluminum structures, often seen at ridiculously low prices, are weak and can be dangerous – an instance where it is better value to pay more.

Whatever greenhouse you choose, ensure that it is erected on and bolted to firm foundations. Much the best flooring is gravel laid over well-firmed soil and if, like many gardeners, you will be growing vegetables, one side of the greenhouse should be allocated for a gravel bed from the start. Removable benches will enable you to use the space given over to vegetables in the winter for other purposes in the summer.

A greenhouse that is not frost-proof in mid-winter is scarcely repaying its investment, for you will be unable even to use it for reliably overwintering dahlia tubers or pelargoniums, let alone for making an early start with your own bedding plants. The structure should be lined with bubble plastic or other insulating material during the winter months, but this on its own will not keep out all frost in most parts of the country.

At the least, you will find that you need to supply sufficient heat to keep the greenhouse frost-free over the winter and spring, up to the time when nature takes over. A paraffin heater is the cheapest type to buy and install and marginally the cheapest to run. But it is tedious and time-consuming to check, clean and fill. A thermostatically controlled electric, oil or gas heater is much more reliable.

An essential adjunct to the greenhouse is a cold frame for hardening off plants before they are placed out in the garden. This is especially important if the plants have been raised in warmth. Most handy gardeners could easily make their own wooden framed structure but simple aluminum types in kit form are freely available. The essential features are a lid that can be opened wide and propped up, and some form of ventilation when the frame is closed.

The lean-to greenhouse (above) makes use of the warmth from the adjoining house wall to enable you to grow winter vegetables, pot plants and even a grapevine, and it can also provide a backdrop to a small paved area for sitting out.

It is almost possible to produce lettuces all year round in a large cold frame (left), although to do this you will need a larger structure than that required simply to harden off transplants.

Garden pools

Nothing brings so much life and interest to a garden as water; but if there are young children in the family it brings dangers too, so anyone in this position should read on, but wait a few years before acting.

A garden pool can either resemble a natural pool or be unashamedly artificial. The semi-natural pool blends imperceptibly into the surrounding garden through the softness of waterside plants at the margins. What I call the unashamedly artificial has hard, stone or tiled margins and sits comfortably in a terrace or other paved area where its surrounding plants are self-contained in pots and tubs. Neither is better than the other but each has its correct placing and looks faintly ridiculous out of it.

There are other constraints to the positioning of any pool: the site requirements are rather like those for a greenhouse – sunny, level ground, away from trees. These will deposit leaves that will rapidly decompose in the water and release gases that can be poisonous both to the plant life and the fish. Sun is essential; the best water plants, such as water lilies, need at least six to eight hours of direct sunlight per day if they are to thrive.

Few people these days line pools with concrete, the choice nowadays lying between a preformed shape of fibreglass or similar substance and synthetic rubber, a material resembling very thick plastic sheeting. The very liberal flexibility in pool shape and contour that synthetic rubber offers makes it my choice every time.

Once your pool is built, restrain your impatience to populate it. Allow about two weeks before the plants, and then about two weeks more before the fish are introduced. And choose both carefully, taking advice from a reputable water garden specialist. All pools need a blend of fish and water snails with submerged plants to provide oxygen, floating plants, such as water lilies, and plants for the shallow margins, but the numbers and types you should choose will vary depending on the surface area and depth of the water.

Fountains

Fountains are a mixed blessing: they enliven the water and help to oxygenate it, but too large a fountain can overchill the water and be detrimental to plants and fish. Whatever type you choose, always employ a qualified electrician to install or check the mechanism and adjust the spray from your fountain so that it is restricted to the center and doesn't cascade over waterlilies, for they are especially resentful of this type of disturbance. It is a good idea to use the same electricity supply in winter for a pool heater to keep a small area free from ice.

Choose water plants with special care. Water lilies (left) are the real essentials but vary enormously in spread and required water depth. The very small pool seen here would be swamped within a season by any other than the pygmy forms. Nonetheless, even a small pool can be home to a group of aquatic irises (above) provided the clump, which will spread naturally, is split up every two or three years.

MAKING A POOL

Whatever type of pool you choose, always ensure that the center is at least 18in preferably 20in deep. This might seem out of proportion if the pool is very small. Nonetheless, it is vital to have this depth of water – quite literally so to the fish who must survive the winter.

Diagrams 1–4 show the stages in making a pool using synthetic rubber sheet – the most adaptable method.

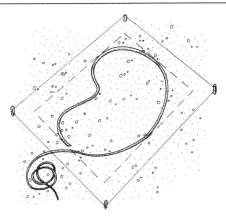

1 Mark out the pool shape with a hose, but allow a generous addition to show the size of rubber sheet.

2 Dig out the pool shape, and layer 2in of sand in the base to provide a smooth bed for the sheet.

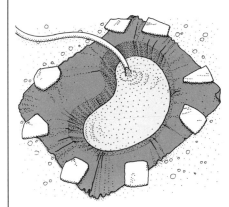

3 Lay the sheet, anchor the edges and fill the hole with water. The sheet stretches to fit the shape.

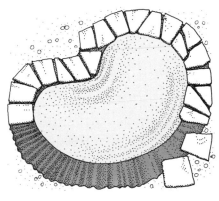

4 Cover the sheet margins with slabs or, for an informal pool, with irregularly shaped stones.

A preformed pool should also be bedded on sand, with more sand used to infill around the sides.

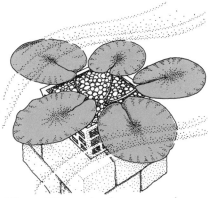

Water lilies and other water plants should be planted in soil in special planting baskets, but never use organic manure or potting mix.

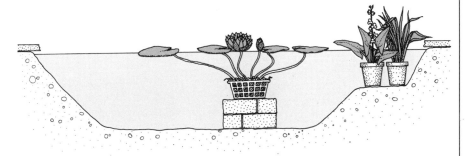

Some plants prefer shallow water, an important reason for having ledges toward the margins. Depth can also be adjusted with blocks.

Containers

Too few gardeners make full use of the opportunities offered by pots, tubs, window boxes, hanging baskets and other containers. Those with limited garden space or no garden at all know of their value, but even the largest garden can benefit from a few carefully placed containers. A well-planted tub will brighten a dull corner and soften a harsh one; it will bring interest to a boring flight of steps or provide an eye-catching feature on a lawn.

Unless you have plenty of under-cover winter storage space and great strength for a twice yearly removal exercise, choose materials that are frost-proof – traditional terracotta pots are not but some modern ones are, so check carefully. Most concrete and reconstituted stone pots are frost-proof but some contain a setting agent that is toxic to plants until the pot is well weathered. Plastic containers are usually frost resistant but they deteriorate after two or three years' exposure to the elements in general.

Much expense can be saved with a little ingenuity. On a short-term basis, almost any type of vessel from halved automobile tires to old plastic pails can be planted, while for an inexpensive large container, nothing betters a wooden half barrel. Ensure that you provide adequate drainage holes and, in the case of wooden tubs, paint the inside with a non-toxic water-based preservative. Wooden baskets treated in this way should last for up to eight years.

Window boxes are best constructed on a two-chamber basis. The outer box should be of painted or treated wood, of the right size and shape to fit the window sill. Inside this, stand plastic troughs and pots, changing them to give you a succession of flowers during the course of the summer.

Soil mixes

There are two important aspects of container gardening that apply to

almost all containers. First, always start with a good quality brand-name potting mix, one that is based on sterile loam, and has a balanced fertilizer content; not garden soil, which may contain a large number of undesirable pests and diseases. Hanging baskets are the exception to this rule; their weight should be kept to a minimum by lining them with sphagnum moss or perforated plastic sheet and filling them with a peat-based potting mix.

It is now possible to buy potting mixes specially formulated for hanging baskets that include a water-retentive gel. You might also like to consider the possibility of having a reserve basket or

two, made up later than the other baskets, and kept in a sheltered spot ready to replace the original baskets toward the end of the summer.

At the start of each season, remove the top 6in or so of old potting mix from large containers, fork a balanced general fertilizer into the remainder and then top up with fresh potting mix. With smaller containers, window boxes and hanging baskets renew all of the potting mix. During the growing season, nutrients will be used up very rapidly and as there is little reserve of soil moisture for the plants to tap, regular watering and fertilizing are essential.

Container gardening is perhaps the most versatile type of all. Even if the individual containers are nothing out of the ordinary, massed together (top left) they can be used to produce what is almost a portable garden or to soften the line at the edge of a path or steps (above). Alternatively, invest in a choice terracotta pot, fill it with particularly striking plants (left) and use it to make a single arresting feature.

Front gardens

Most gardeners would be less than honest if they didn't admit that the reward for at least part of their gardening endeavor comes from presenting an attractive vision to neighbors and passers-by. This means that it is worth devoting a little special care and thought to your front garden, assuming that you have one, always bearing in mind the relationship between what you wish to attempt and the time you have to spare.

If you have a great deal of time, then your front garden can be filled with beds and borders, with herbaceous perennials and bedding annuals, chosen, planted, staked, tied, watered, fed, dead-headed and possibly replaced right through the summer. Whatever the week or month, passers-by will be rewarded with a stunning display. But most of us are not blessed with so much time and our front gardens of beds and borders would almost certainly look sad for a long proportion of the year. In this case, it is wiser to opt for simplicity.

If the garden is sufficiently large, fill it with lawn; if not, have a graveled or attractively paved yard. Within the lawn or yard, plant a few truly choice small trees or specimen shrubs. The predominant color therefore will be cool green and you can superimpose splashes of brightness and color upon this with a few carefully planted and tended tubs, window boxes or hanging baskets. Keep a few plants in reserve so that any deficiencies or defects that arise during the course of the summer can swiftly be rectified.

Keep the gravel raked, the paving swept or the lawn mown (and, most importantly, well edged), and you will have not only the much greater peace of mind that comes from knowing that things are not 'getting on top of you' but you will be assured that your garden is presenting at least one attractive face to the outside world.

Even houses that front more or less directly onto a street should not be neglected. Hanging baskets, window boxes and climbing plants can be used to enhance a house wall but, when choosing any plants to grow so close to the house itself, give just a moment's thought to the color scheme of the house and choose flowers that will harmonize with it.

More than any other part of your garden, the front should be planned to allow for the time that you have available. A well-tended lawn, flowering trees and a few carefully selected bulbs or perennials (top left) can be guaranteed to be labor saving yet look attractive for much of the year. On a smaller scale, the tiny yard garden (left), with a few containers and well-chosen plants, always presents a neat and tidy appearance, but the evocative informality of the traditional cottage (above) will soon deteriorate into chaos without fairly constant attention.

Part 3

PLANTS AND PLANTING

Choosing plants and planting them in the garden is one of the most pleasant aspects of gardening – though by no means as simple as it may at first appear to be – but ensuring that young plants survive to maturity offers a considerable challenge. The modern horticultural industry presents us with prepacked vegetation of all kinds, expertly raised and marketed. There is still, however, an advantage in knowing, before visiting the garden supply store or nursery, how to judge which are the good and which the not so good among the plants, which are simple and interesting to raise ourselves (and therefore a waste of money to buy) and which are difficult and better bought 'ready made'. What is the best time of year to buy shrubs, bedding plants or vegetable transplants and exactly how should they all be treated when we arrive home? Not all plants should be planted in the same way, to the same depth or at the same spacing. How can you increase your stock of favorite garden plants and go about exchanging them with friends and neighbors? Should you collect seed from them or take cuttings? What are the secrets of ensuring that all seeds germinate successfully? You certainly don't need to be an expert botanist to be a gardener, but knowing just a little of what makes up a plant and of how it lives its life will help you to overcome some of the gardening difficulties that all of us face from time to time.

Every garden must have its plants but the matter of whether any individual is better bought as a plant, raised from seed, or multiplied by division, cuttings or other means should be given careful thought.

Plant anatomy

As every school child knows, a plant can be divided basically into roots, stems, leaves, flowers and fruit. In most types of plant, these parts are distinct and readily recognizable, although it is the fact that they are modified in various ways that gives rise to the enormous and wonderful diversity in appearance throughout the plant kingdom as a whole. The 'flower' of a rose, for example, is a single entity, whereas that of a buddleia is a mass of small individual blooms. Even a daisy, dahlia or chrysanthemum flower head is actually made up of many small individual flowers. Roots, stems and leaves are usually fairly self-evident but cactus spines are actually modified leaves, bulbs are modified underground buds, and tubers are enlarged underground fleshy stems. Moreover, although most stems appear above ground and most roots below it, some types of stems such as rhizomes are subterranean and some plants, like *Monstera* or the many orchid species that come originally from steamy tropical forests, may have at least some roots dangling from many feet up in the air. All is not necessarily exactly what it seems.

Food requirements

There are some sound aspects of practical gardening to be learned from a little knowledge of plant anatomy and plant function. A plant, like any other living organism, needs both nutrients and water but it differs from animals and other living things in that it is able to manufacture its own food requirements from the basic raw materials of carbon dioxide and water. It achieves this through photosynthesis, by trapping the energy in sunlight with the aid of chlorophyll, the green pigments that most plants possess.

Thus, garden plants need light and air, but some have adapted to grow in lower light levels than others. Such plants, occurring naturally in the deep shade of woodlands for instance, will grow in apparently inhospitable, dark parts of the garden but will not thrive in the bright sunshine that others require. All of which makes it essential to check the conditions that particular plants need before introducing them to your garden, so avoiding the disappointment of plants failing.

The stem of a plant acts mainly to hold the energy trapping leaves in a position where they will function most efficiently, but the underground roots have a dual function. In part, they are present to anchor a plant firmly in one spot (and remember that few garden plants will have the chance to grow satisfactorily if they are physically unstable) but they are also there to enable the plant to extract the water and mineral nutrients from the soil.

This is why we normally apply fertilizer to the soil, although plants can also take up a small amount of liquid through their leaves – a feature that we can make use of during the summer growing season by spraying them with liquid fertilizer and thus ensuring that the nutrient is delivered where it is needed very rapidly indeed.

Most people know that flowers are the plant's reproductive structures and that they ultimately develop into seed-bearing organs called fruits. Nonetheless, many of our most attractive garden ornamentals never set seeds for they have been carefully selected to bear double flowers – blooms in which the reproductive stamens and other parts have been converted into more petals. As a result, plants of this type must either be tricked back by a plant breeding specialist into producing at least a few stamens or they must be propagated in other ways, such as by cuttings.

All is not what it seems in the plant kingdom: the yellow flowers of the fremontodendron, for instance, are colored, not by the petals but by the sepals.

ANATOMY OF A PLANT

Because plants vary so much in their structure, it is difficult to choose an example that can really be said to typify the flowering plant in all respects. Nonetheless this sweet violet illustrates many of the important features. It is clearly divided into flowers (1), each on a flower stalk (2), the leaves (3), each with their own stalk (4), a stem (5) – in this instance rather reduced to a short, stubby structure – and the underground roots (6). The roots include both fleshy and fibrous types, while running close to the soil surface are underground stems or rhizomes (7), each with small clusters of leaves arising from joints or nodes (8).

The structure of the flower is typical of many pollinated by insects in having the pollen-bearing stamens (9) well protected within the petals (10) which in this instance form a tubular structure. Around the petals are the green, rather leaf-like sepals (11) and within, in addition to the stamens, the pollen-receiving stigma (12) is visible above the ovary (13). After being pollinated, the ovary develops to form the fruit (14) within which seeds (15), here shown four times life size, are borne.

Where will your plants come from?

In general, a plant is best bought and planted in its most robust form. Seeds, bulbs, corms, and tubers are all designed to enable a plant to survive during the adverse conditions of the winter or during a summer 'resting' period but they are also convenient and durable 'packages', made full use of by suppliers and gardeners alike. All the same, it is sometimes impossible or nonsensical to obtain a plant in such a form – buying trees as seeds, for instance, is an option for the very patient gardener only, while in other cases, we may not have adequate facilities to carry out the entire raising operation ourselves. In such instances, we are dependent on the skill of the plant producer and retailer to grow, package and offer the plant in a well-protected form and with a high degree of certainty that it will thrive and easily become established when planted.

Seeds can be bought either through mail order or over the counter. In general, a mail order catalog offers a considerably larger range of plants and varieties than is present in a local store, although you may find that the larger garden supply stores stock a sufficiently wide range for your needs. The disadvantage of mail order purchase is that you must decide on your requirements several months in advance. Bulbs too can be bought by mail order and this is almost essential if you want any other than the most popular types. Also, it is possible to buy the more common bulbs in bulk much more cheaply at a garden supply store.

No garden supply store, seed merchant or mail order plant supplier raises all of their own plants – the ranges of types and varieties required are just too large. Some plants are inherently difficult to propagate or are

A garden supply store is the best overall source of supply for plants and equipment, but shop around for one that also offers sound advice.

not amenable to easy transportation and are best produced by specialists with years of accumulated expertise. Almost all of the best tulip bulbs, for instance, are grown in Holland, whereas small specialized nurseries may produce most of the unusual varieties of Japanese maples sold in this country. All the same, there is much to be said for patronizing a garden supply store that has at least a small nursery attached to or associated with it, demonstrating that the company has some sound knowledge about plants and their requirements (which may well not be true of your local supermarket or a chain store).

Garden supply stores

The plants in a garden supply store should appear well furnished with leaves, with no dead shoots or obvious disease lesions; their roots should be well covered by moist potting mix; they should be in pots free from extensive weed or moss growth, and arranged in meaningful and helpful groups – plants for shade, or ground cover plants for sunny places, for instance. Every plant (not merely the rack or batch) should be individually and fully labeled and terms of a guarantee should be displayed prominently. Take special care when buying plants grown in containers. Roots should not be crowded into an undersized pot: once root binding has begun, it is difficult to correct and it may adversely affect the plant later in its life. Therefore always check the root system of a plant, especially a woody plant, before buying. The staff must have a good working knowledge of plant husbandry – if they can't give convincing answers to your queries, then shop elsewhere, and if you are sold a plant that turns out to be an incorrect variety it should be exchanged without question. Even if the plant simply fails to grow, most reputable garden supply stores will replace it.

PLANTING TECHNIQUES

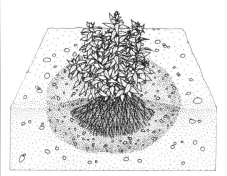

Herbaceous perennials – carefully trim away dead or damaged roots and shoots, pull out any weeds from within the clump and dust the planting hole with bonemeal.

Bare-rooted plants – use a hole at least 4in wider than the roots' spread, arrange them carefully and firm around with 10 per cent peat or humus and a handful of bonemeal.

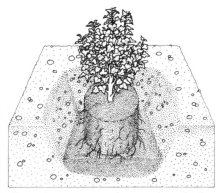

Container-grown plants – knock the plant from its container, gently tease out the roots at the edges and firm around with peat or humus and a handful of bonemeal.

Sowing seeds

It is immensely satisfying to raise at least some plants from seed collected in your own garden. Provided that you avoid collecting from F₁ hybrid varieties – this will be marked on the original seed packet – whose seed gives rise to a useless hotch-potch of plants, home collected seed certainly has the attractive attribute of cheapness; but at first it is wise to place yourself mainly in the safe hands of the seed companies and their packeted products.

Nothing compares with the taste of the vegetable that you have nurtured from brown 'dust', through babyhood to juvenility and maturity. Certainly, all vegetables can and should be raised from seed. Many are sown directly in the garden each year, while others are best transplanted out as young seedlings. Among flowering ornamentals, annual bedding plants can be bought as transplant sized youngsters but all are simple to raise yourself if you have the space. Some border perennials can be raised from seed too, but the varieties available are limited and often not the best – in most instances, it is better to buy young plants and multiply them by cuttings or division in subsequent seasons.

Sowing methods

Seeds are sown in one of two main ways – either in the spring or occasionally in the fall directly into the positions in the garden in which the adult plant is to grow, or into a seedling potting mix in some form of propagator for transplanting later. The normal practice with some annual flowers and most vegetables is to sow directly, although in some cases (and if you have room) it is possible to obtain earlier crops and earlier flowers by raising the plants in the greenhouse or other protection first. In a few instances and with the very hardiest plants, like spinach or pansies, for example, seed can actually be sown outdoors in the fall of the previous year to give the plants a head

The lovely seeds and fruits of plants such as lunaria (top) or skimmia (above) are the objects of their cultivation. But you can allow other plants to set seed too. Lupins for instance seed freely and offer the chance of obtaining plants with color variations. The lupin seedling (left) shows the distinction between the fleshy seed leaves or cotyledons which emerge first, and the true leaves that follow.

start on the season.

Plants, like sweet peppers and eggplants among vegetables or pelargoniums and impatiens among flowers, must be sown and raised under protection until the danger of frost is passed. If these plants were sown directly outdoors in early summer, they would not have a long enough period to grow to maturity before the fall, so look carefully on your seed packet and/or in the catalog to see how your chosen plants should be managed.

Modern seed packets give you other valuable advice which can help you to avoid disappointment. The first thing to check is the time recommended for sowing. Some plants take a long time to germinate and/or grow. Sweet peppers and eggplants grow more slowly than tomatoes for instance and must be sown earlier, while pelargoniums need about four months from sowing to planting out if they are to flower effectively early in the summer. Second, check on any special procedures needed to ensure or assist germination. Some seeds, for example, will not germinate if they are buried and these should be sown on the surface of the seedling potting mix, sometimes this is because light is needed to stimulate their germination but more often it is because, as with lobelia, the seeds are so small that their food reserves are inadequate for a seedling plant to grow up to the daylight. Other seeds, like parsnip and celery, are notoriously slow or erratic in germination and a technique like fluid sowing will help enormously.

Germination

Check also that you are offering the seeds the correct germination temperature. Most germinate satisfactorily over a fairly wide range with an optimum around 65°F but some, like nemesia, are inhibited at this relatively high temperature, whereas others,

SOWING SEEDS

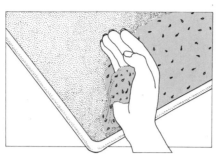

To help uniform sowing of very tiny seeds, such as bedding begonias, mix the seeds with very fine sand or brick dust and scatter this evenly over the potting mix.

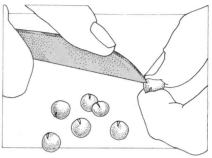

Some hard-coated seeds, like certain sweet pea varieties, will germinate best if they are nicked carefully with the point of a sharp knife on the side away from the 'eye'.

FLUID SOWING

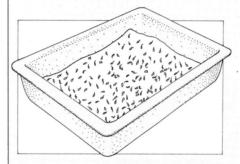

1 Scatter the seeds evenly on damp tissue in a lunch box or other closed container and then keep it in a warm place until most of the seeds have germinated.

2 Carefully remove with forceps any ungerminated seeds and then gently wash the remainder from the tissue into a fine kitchen sieve under running water.

3 Stir the germinated seeds into a bowl either of ready prepared dilute cellulose wallpaper paste (not containing any fungicide) or brand-name sowing gel.

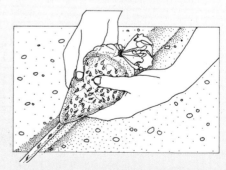

4 Place the seed and gel mixture into a plastic bag, cut off one corner, squeeze it into seedling potting mix or a drill in the garden, and then cover in the usual way.

such as salvias, require even greater warmth. A few seeds, such as alstroemerias, need a spell at high temperature, followed by a spell in the refrigerator and then a return to high temperature again. Your seed packet should reveal all, but it is worth adding that the bottom of a refrigerator makes an excellent storage place for seed packets in general, provided it is dry. Kept in this way, most seeds will remain viable for two years at least.

There are a few more golden rules. When sowing seeds into flats or propagators, always ensure that the container has been well washed out beforehand, dipped in a brand-name garden disinfectant and then rinsed in clean water; and always use fresh potting mix. Sow thinly; a common mistake is to sow far too many seeds, both into propagators and directly into the garden, where the plants will compete with each other to their mutual detriment. Remember that seeds need moisture to germinate and the flat or propagator must be covered at first, but once emerged, the seedling needs ventilation too if it isn't to succumb to fungal diseases.

Once the seedlings have their true leaves (not the cotyledons or seed leaves which are the first to emerge), they should be pricked on into further flats and grown on to transplanting size. If you have used a seedling potting mix initially, you will need a potting mix for the transplants as this has a different blend of fertilizers. Simpler for most types of plant is to use a multipurpose or universal mix for both jobs but *always* use fresh each time.

Hardening off

The third and equally important stage is hardening off. This is a procedure by which plants are accustomed gradually to the rigors of the great outdoors. Raised in the warmth of the greenhouse or on the kitchen window sill, their tissues will be soft and sappy and

PROPAGATORS

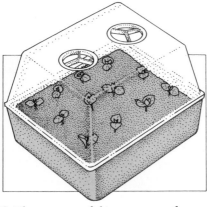

1 The simple transparent plastic cover for a plant pot is useful as an aid for rooting cuttings.

2 The most useful propagator for general sowing and cuttings is a ventilated cover over a seed flat.

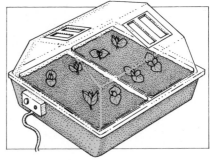

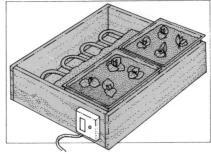

3 With an electric heater in the base, this propagator offers much more rapid and certain germination.

4 A sand bench, containing heating cables over which flats are placed, offers the greatest versatility.

PRICKING OUT SEEDLINGS

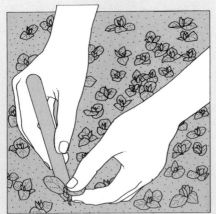

Remove seedlings very carefully from potting mix with a small kitchen fork or a metal widger.

When handling seedlings, pick them up by holding a leaf, not the stem which is more easily crushed.

prone to damage from drying winds, scorching sun or cold drafts (and for this reason, always ask if transplants that you buy have been hardened off). For hardening off, you will need a cold frame—a simple device with a glazed lid that can be opened in the daytime but closed down for protection at night. After about seven to ten days of this regime, the top can be left open all of the time (other than on the very coldest night), for a further week or so before the transplants are finally placed in their permanent positions.

Cloches

A cloche is something of a greenhouse in miniature and it serves the valuable function of giving just that little extra protection from wind and cold that enables plants to be planted a few weeks earlier in the season than normal and, of course, results in slightly earlier flowers and vegetables. But there is another use for the cloche, the most neglected use of all: place cloches a week or so in advance over the prepared bed into which seeds are to be sown or transplants planted. This will have the valuable effect of warming the soil, enhancing seed germination and ensuring that transplants are not given the shock of being thrust into cold soil.

A cold frame (above) provides an ideal place to harden off bedding plants before they are planted. Cloches (right) can be used not only to lengthen the growing season at the beginning and end, but also to offer a means of growing some plants, such as these lettuces, right through the winter.

PROTECTING PLANTS

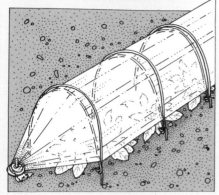

The cheapest and simplest form of continuous cloche is made from plastic stretched over wire hoops.

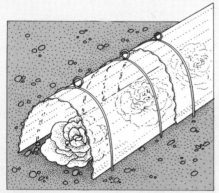

Rather more robust is flexible transparent corrugated plastic sheet, held firm with metal pegs.

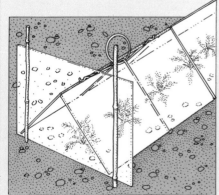

Glass cloches with metal frames can be linked end to end: they retain heat very well but are expensive.

Bulbs, corms and tubers

Although botanically quite different, bulbs, corms and tubers are grown in rather similar ways. Bulbs are the food stores produced by such popular plants as daffodils, tulips, snowdrops, some irises, lilies, hyacinths, crown imperials and scillas. Corms fulfil a similar role for crocuses, gladioli and cyclamen among others, while tubers are formed most notably by dahlias. An additional and related structure is the rhizome, the thick, fleshy creeping stem that is produced by bearded and related types of iris.

Many bulbous plants are dormant or resting during the summer (think of all those that flower in spring and then 'disappear'), and so are normally bought and planted in the fall. A few, rather sadly neglected among the many other summer flowering garden plants, bloom later and are available for planting in the spring. Among these are dahlias, tuberous begonias, naked ladies (*Lychoris*), tuberoses and gladioli.

All bulbs should be planted as soon as possible after purchase. A good general maxim is to plant them with the base of the bulb at a depth in the soil equal to roughly two and a half times the bulb's diameter. To minimize the likelihood of rotting, soak bulbs for about half an hour before planting in a spray-strength mixture of systemic fungicide (use rubber gloves to protect your hands).

After flowering

None of the summer- and fall-flowering bulbs except lilies are hardy, that is they cannot be left permanently in the ground. They must therefore be lifted each fall and then stored carefully until spring. To dry bulbs, arrange them well spaced out on trays or in shallow boxes and lightly air dry in a cool airy frost-free location. When their surfaces have dried, place the bulbs in a rodent-proof box filled with dry sawdust or vermiculite and return to the cool airy location.

If you find this procedure troublesome, concentrate on growing the easy spring-flowering bulbs such as snowdrops and squills, whose foliage dies back quite early in the season. The fact that these hardy bulbs can be left in the ground, however, does not mean they should be left entirely to their own devices. After flowering, the plant must be given every encouragement to build up its bulb again for the following year. The best way to do this is to cut off the old flower and to fertilize lightly. The foliage can be cut back six weeks after flowering as it begins to yellow. Do not be tempted to cut back

Bulbs used in repeated masses of color and form can have a dramatic impact on the garden – spring or summer.

the foliage too soon, because this will weaken the bulb, and fewer flowers will be produced next year.

If you do not want dying foliage to detract from the other plants in the bed, lift the bulbs carefully after flowering and then replant or 'heel' them in somewhere else in the garden where they can die down naturally. Then lift and dry them for replanting in the fall.

CROCUS ON BED OF SAND

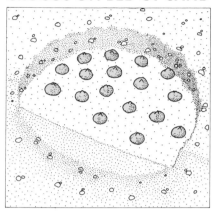

Even in well-drained soil all bulbs and corms will benefit from being planted on sand to minimize rotting.

CROCUS WITH NETTING

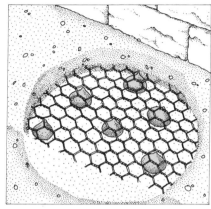

To deter mice and voles, plant deeper and lay fine chicken wire over corms below the soil surface.

GLADIOLUS CORMS

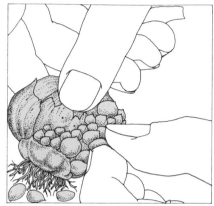

When lifting gladioli, keep the baby cormlets and pot them up separately in the spring.

LAYERED DAFFODILS

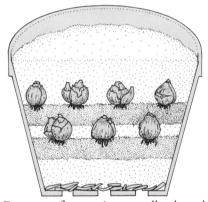

For more flowers in a small tub and to prolong the flowering season, plant the bulbs in two layers.

DEEP PLANTED DWARF IRIS

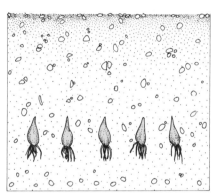

Dwarf bulbous irises are usually more likely to flower again in future years if planted 6in deep.

SURFACE AND DEEP LILY

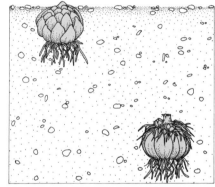

Most lilies are planted 6in to 8in deep but the Madonna lily should lie only just below the surface.

FRITILLARIA ON SIDE

The crown imperial bulb should be planted on its side to prevent water collecting and stop rotting.

DAFFODILS UNDER TURF

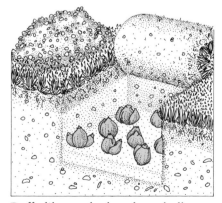

Daffodils are the best large bulbs to naturalize in grass but should be planted about 8in deep.

DAHLIA AND STAKE

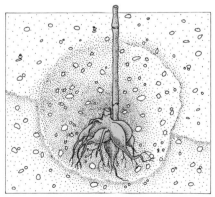

When a stake is needed with fleshy-rooted plants, put it in at planting time to minimize damage.

Cuttings and division

While seeds provide the obvious means for plants to reproduce themselves naturally, one of the great joys of gardening is in being able to short-cut the natural process and multiply your plants very much more rapidly.

Division

The easiest method of all is by division – simply slicing or pulling one plant into several parts, each of which is then planted. Not all plants are amenable to this somewhat crude but effective technique and it is most valuable with herbaceous perennials such as asters, black-eyed susans or hardy geraniums. Plants can be divided in fall or in the spring, just as growth is starting.

Small clumps can be pulled apart by hand but two forks are needed for large ones. Discard the dead, worn-out area in the center and use the peripheral parts to start afresh. Woody plants do not normally respond to division, and care is needed too with plants such as peonies that have large, fleshy roots. It is very difficult to avoid damaging at least some roots on these plants and the cut surfaces should be dusted with a fungicide such as sulfur or benomyl to minimize the likelihood of rotting.

Cuttings

A cutting is more or less what its name suggests; a small part cut from a mature plant and induced to form roots. It is a bland name that disguises one of the most exciting, easy and fascinating aspects in all of gardening. Most plants have the potential to form new roots in this way, and, depending on the type of plant, the cutting can be taken from other roots, from soft stems, slightly harder stems, woody stems or leaves. Indeed, the flowers and the fruit are almost the only parts that do not respond satisfactorily. Largely because of the seasonal availability of the raw material, different types of cutting are taken at different times of the year – softwood and leaf cuttings usually in

CUTTINGS: SOFTWOOD

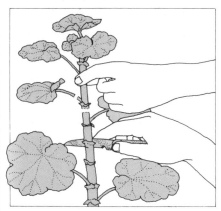

1 Take pelargonium cuttings from just below a leaf joint but always trim the plant back to the next joint.

2 Remove the lowest leaves, dip the shoot into rooting powder and insert it into moist rooting medium.

Dahlias are easy – take strong shoots 3in to 4in long from tubers brought into warmth in the spring.

SEMI-HARDWOOD

1 Heeled cuttings of rosemary are taken by *pulling* off a side shoot with a sliver of wood at the base.

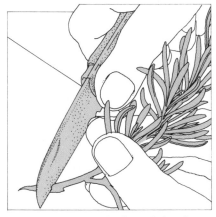

2 Trim the ragged edge of the sliver or heel and dip the end into rooting powder.

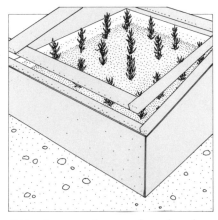

3 Sand, or a mixture of sand and peat, makes a good rooting medium for cuttings but must be kept moist,

HARDWOOD

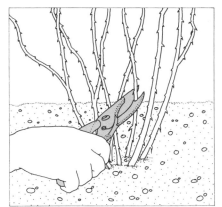

1 Most rose cuttings are easy to root – take them from long, ripe, straight and healthy shoots in late fall.

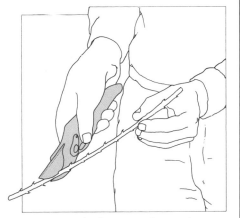

2 Trim each shoot to about 8in. (Incidentally, a rose from cuttings will give no trouble with suckers.)

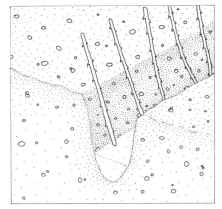

3 Place them slightly slanting on a bed of sand in a slit trench dug outdoors in a sheltered spot.

Asters are easily divided in the spring or fall; Aster frikartii *is the best and most disease free of all the varieties.*

spring and early summer, semi-hardwood a little later, hardwood during the dormant period in late fall and root cuttings in the winter.

While root and leaf cuttings are self-explanatory, the differences between the types of stem cutting may not be. A softwood cutting is taken from a soft, fairly fleshy shoot such as the young growth on a dahlia plant; if bent between the fingers, it will snap. A semi-hardwood cutting is from a shoot that has begun to harden slightly, like an azalea in mid-summer; the shoots are

DIVISION

Small clumps of herbaceous plants can be pulled apart but use two forks to separate large ones.

Two plants that are easy to multiply by root cuttings are the border phlox (above) and the Californian tree poppy (right). For phlox, take ½in root cuttings in early spring; harden them off when the shoots are 2in to 3in high, and transplant them to permanent positions in the summer of the following year. For tree poppies, take 3in root cuttings, again in early spring, or dig up and replant any suckers growing at a distance from the original plant.

readily pliable between the fingers. A hardwood cutting is from a truly woody shoot or stem but usually before it has become very hard and 'twiggy'.

Hardwood cuttings are usually placed in soil outdoors while all other types are normally grown (or 'struck') in light potting mix in a greenhouse or cold frame. When taking any cutting that bears leaves, remember that it will lose water through those leaves, but because it has no roots it will be unable to make up this loss from the potting mix. The cuttings must therefore be kept in a moist atmosphere to minimize the danger of drying out. A propagator with a cover is ideal, and the heated type will speed rooting at the same time by keeping the potting mix warm. Rooting is also aided, certainly in all except root and hardwood cuttings, by dipping the leaf or shoot in a rooting powder containing hormone-like chemicals. Rooting powders also generally contain a fungicide which helps lessen the likelihood of the cuttings rotting.

When cuttings have rooted, contain your inevitable enthusiasm – many are moved on too quickly and fail to survive this ordeal. After rooting, transplant cuttings into individual pots of potting mix and grow them on for at least six months to enable them to build up a sound root system before planting them in their permanent positions in the garden.

There are some shrubs that rarely form roots from cuttings, but many of these can be propagated by layering. Select a low growing branch and pull it down to soil level. Bend it so that there is a slight split on the underside, then cover this part with soil and either weigh down the whole with a brick or a metal peg made from a clothes hanger. Roots should form within about two years, after which the young plant can be severed from its parent and transplanted elsewhere in the garden.

LEAF AND ROOT CUTTINGS

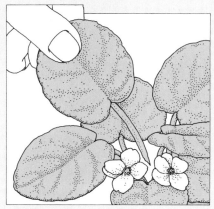

1 Pull a healthy leaf from the outer part of an African violet plant, taking care to leave no stub.

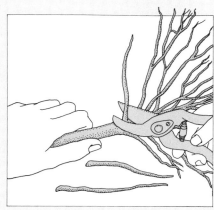

1 Choose firm, healthy roots of roughly pencil thickness and trim off lengths of about 2in to 3in.

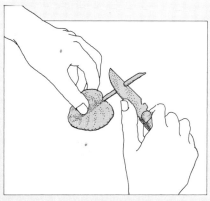

2 Trim away the ragged end, taking care to cut away from you and onto a board.

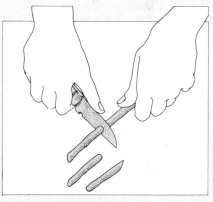

2 Trim the root lengths carefully and give each a straight cut at the top and a slanting cut at the base.

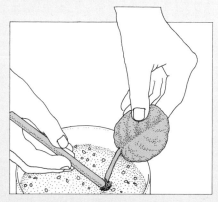

3 Use a dibble to make a hole for the cutting. Those put around the edge of the pot are less likely to rot.

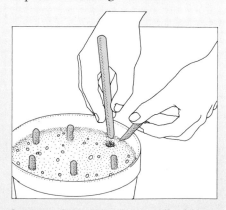

3 Insert the cuttings vertically for their full length or lay them flat and just cover them with potting mix.

Part 4

PLANTING DESIGNS

When you visit one of the great botanic gardens that are open to the public, there is a good chance that you will be filled with admiration at the splendid displays. There is also a good chance that when you return to your own garden you will be somewhat downhearted and feel that yours could never match what you have seen, but this is simply not the case. For what is it about a great or even a very good garden that distinguishes it and sets it apart from the average? Certainly not the size, for some of the loveliest and best gardens are very small city plots. Not the weed control and the healthy plants either, for anyone can use a hoe or apply weedkiller and fertilizer. Not even the types of plant, for while some may be rare, exotic and expensive, there are countless other beautiful and rewarding species that are inexpensive and freely available. No, it is almost entirely due to the way that the plants are put together and the way in which the garden is divided into borders, beds, shrubberies and other areas. And this is something that you can achieve too. There is nothing magical about making a beautiful garden: it is a combination of a little forethought and a little patience, together with a willingness to adapt other people's successful ideas to the circumstances of your own garden.

Ultimately, a garden is the way that someone has put plants together: color preferences vary from individual to individual, but the planting design should always be a deliberate expression of personal style; not left to chance.

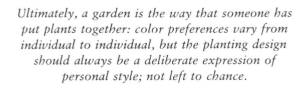

Mixed borders

The mixed border offers more ornamental value in return for effort than any other part of the modern garden. An immensely versatile feature, it can be tailored to the size and shape of almost any garden (other, perhaps, than the very tiny).

The essential ingredients of a mixed border are herbaceous perennials, bulbs and shrubs, sometimes with an additional sprinkling of annuals and biennials, and this blend is very largely a feature of the modern, twentieth-century garden. By the late nineteenth century, most gardens had large borders containing almost exclusively herbaceous perennials. But while geraniums, delphiniums and their like have the delightful advantage of coming up from the ground year after year, they have limited flowering periods, and even the cleverest gardeners, with almost limitless assistance, found it extremely difficult to obtain plantings that gave continuity of color and interest through the summer. Gardeners had to resort to moving plants into and out of the border in pots to fill in the gaps. This was labor intensive, and the simpler modern solution is to have a permanent framework of shrubs, always in leaf, of attractive overall shape and often with the added bonus of flowers of their own. Between the shrubs can come the herbaceous perennials and among them bulbs and annuals.

If at all possible, clear a border completely before starting to plant. This will enable you to remove thoroughly and carefully all perennial weeds and to dig in (preferably by double digging) generous additions of compost or manure. The border will not be dug again in its entirety for a very long time indeed and so it is worth doing the task properly.

A mixed border is rather like a chess board: a few positions – the castles, the king and the queen – can be identified and fixed fairly readily. The other

major components – the bishops and the knights – are likely to require moving to some extent after a year or two, while the smaller members, the pawns, may well need periodic adjustment. The overall shape should be rather like that of an array of chessmen too – taller at the back (and especially toward the center), graduating gently to the smaller plants at the front and sides of the border.

Depending on the actual dimensions of your border, the shape could be that of a single set of chessmen or of two or more arranged side by side, with two or more groups of taller plantings rather than one in the center.

Woody plants

First, consider the choice of castles, king and queen. For the castles, at either end of the border and toward the back, you need fairly fast growing shrubs that are amenable to pruning and can readily be maintained at a height of three to four feet. Although they must offer year-round interest, this doesn't necessarily mean they must be evergreen; their winter shape, bark or even winter flowers on bare shoots will provide this admirably. Among the possibilities that you might consider are the shrubby dogwood with red winter stems, *Cornus alba* Sibirica, one of the shrubby willows

like *Salix melanostachys* or *S. helvetica*, which is enlivened by attractive buds and/or catkins, or a Chinese witch hazel, *Hamamelis mollis*, with scented winter blossoms.

For the kings and queens at the center back, choose especially carefully. Depending on the overall size of your border, this could be a tall shrub or a small tree. In many respects, a small tree is better, for the lower part must be tolerant of the shade that will be supplied by the surrounding herbaceous plants. But it must not, in turn, cast dense shade itself when in leaf. One of my ideals is Korean stewartia, which has beautiful camellia-like flowers in

the summer and a smooth mottled bark to provide an attractive feature in the winter. Also the shadbush, *Amelanchier canadensis*, is a delightful tree for a border, offering a delicate tracery of twigs in winter, gentle white blossom in spring, small, dainty foliage through the summer and a glorious fall color.

The plants that fill in around these cores should also include some shrubs, but lower growing types are needed here. Potentillas are excellent border shrubs, giving flowers over a very long period in summer, but among many, many others are dwarf weigela, low growing shrub roses like Frau Dagmar

The great joy of planting and making a mixed border is that there are very few rules. If a mixture of yellow achilleas, blue campanulas and pinky purple geraniums (above) appeals to you, then there is no reason why you should not choose them. Perhaps the most important aspect to remember is that time passes from month to month; the small border (left) for instance, with golden alyssum, thrift and irises will be lovely in June, but is there space for plants to continue the interest throughout the summer?

PLAN FOR A MIXED BORDER

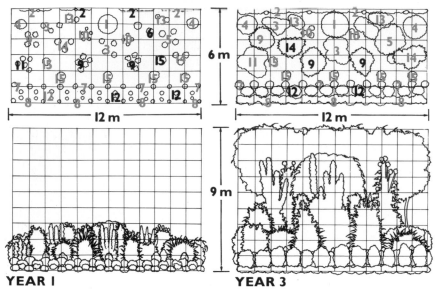

6 m

12 m

12 m

9 m

YEAR 1

YEAR 3

BORDER IN SUMMER OF YEAR 3

1 *Buddleia alternifolia*
2 *Clemetis montana*
3 *Delphinium* Pacific Giant
4 *Salix helvetica*
5 Peonies
6 Lupins
7 Miniature roses
8 *Aubrieta*
9 Day lilies
10 Lilies
11 Chinese lantern plant
12 *Potentilla* Day Dawn
13 *Echinops ritro*
14 *Phalaris arundinacea variegata*
   (Gardener's garters)
15 Dwarf conifers

This is a plan for a typical mixed border shown in July of its third year. The mini-plans above show the original planting plan (left) and the degree of spread after three years (right). It might seem ultra-critical to point out errors in an attractive border like this one, that appears so well planned and organized. The ground is well covered and there is plenty of bloom, but on the other hand you can see from the ground plans above that some plants have grown at a much faster rate than the gardener expected, with the result that a few of his plants have disappeared beneath larger ones. Never mind, this is all part of the fun of gardening, and in the fall there will be time to rescue plants, like the miniature roses, that have been overshadowed and to thin out others, like the Chinese lantern plants, that have grown particularly quickly.

Hastrup or Cécile Brunner, modern miniature roses such as Magic Carousel and, for the front, more or less prostrate evergreen plants such as *Euonymus fortunei.*

Herbaceous perennials

So much for the woody structure of the border. In between, come all of the familiar herbaceous perennials – sunflowers, day lilies, sedums, asters, campanulas, heleniums, phlox, aconitums, irises; all plants that you remember from your childhood and that conjure up images of summers long gone, endless, lazy and unfailingly warm. A good catalog or a good garden supply store label will guide you with their placing. Certainly the very tall plants like perennial sunflowers, some of the achilleas and globe thistles should go at the back, the medium sized plants like many of the hardy geraniums should be in the middle and the low growing types like hostas and sedums at the front. But the real thrill of mixed border gardening comes as you learn a little more each season. No matter that you underestimated the spread of a hosta, forgot that there is little left of a delphinium once the flowers are over, watched a potentilla vanish before your eyes under the shade of peonies or wondered why no-

The different possible combinations of plants for the mixed border are almost limitless. In many instances, the only way to discover new and original ones is by your own experimentation. In not more than one garden in ten thousand will anyone have planted Crocosmia masonorum *with golden juniper and rudbeckia (left) or yellow winter hazel* Corylopsis pauciflora *with the red-stemmed dogwood,* Cornus alba Sibirica *(above). No-one would ever suggest these mixtures to you, yet the effects are magical.*

SOME HERBACEOUS PERENNIALS FOR SPECIAL CONDITIONS

Heavy, clay soils	Wet, boggy soils	Dry, sunny sites	Shady sites
Alchemilla (lady's mantle)	Acorus	Acaena (New Zealand burr)	Aconitum (monk's hood)
Bergenia	Astilbe	Achillea (yarrow)	Ajuga
Brunnera	Caltha (marsh marigold)	Antennaria	Alchemilla (lady's mantle)
Caltha (marsh marigold)	Filipendula	Arabis	Anemone nemorosa (wood
Geranium	Hemerocallis (day lily)	Armeria (thrift)	anemone)
Hemerocallis (day lily)	Inula	Artemisia	Aquilegia (columbine)
Hosta	Iris kaempferi	Aubrieta	Astilbe
Inula	Lysichitum	Crocosmia	Bergenia
Lamium (dead nettle)	Lythrum	Dianthus (pinks and	Convallaria
Liriope	Myosotis (forget-me-not)	carnations)	Digitalis (foxglove)
Vinca	Polygonum	Dimorphotheca (Cape	Epimedium
	Many primulas	marigold)	Some geraniums
	Trollius (globe flower)	Echinops (globe thistle)	Helleborus
		Erodium (stork's bill)	Hepatica
		Eryngium	Hosta
		Many euphorbias	Lamium (dead nettle)
		Helianthemum (rock rose)	Lysimachia
		Lavandula (lavender)	Omphalodes
		Oenothera	Polygonum
		Paeonia (peony)	Some primulas
		Papaver (poppy)	Pulmonaria
		Phlomis	Teucrium
		Perouskia	Viola
		Potentilla	
		Rudbeckia	
		Saponaria	
		Sedum	
		Senecio	
		Thymus (thyme)	

one told you about the invasiveness of the Chinese lantern plant. There is no perfect border nor ever will be. It is what you or I make it and its pleasure is to be measured in the satisfaction of blending colors, flowering times, heights, widths and shapes to create a four-dimensional painting.

The mass of plant growth that makes

Too often, the border is forgotten after July, yet the fall colors of Sedum spectabile, *veronicas, phlox, green fennel and other late season plants are as lovely as anything that high summer can offer.*

up a border in the height of summer has a prodigious demand for water and the easiest way to supply this is by laying a length of perforated irrigation hose through the bed early in the season. All you need do after this is to connect one end to your hose to deliver a gentle rain. It is also important that the soil between the plants is well mulched, for this will not only help maintain a soil in moist condition, but will suppress weed growth until the plants have developed the leaf cover to do this themselves. Feed the border each fall with a balanced fertilizer. Finally — my strongest maxim —

stake all tall plants early, before the flop sets in. And in staking early, there should be no need to stake often, for modern brand-name interlocking metal stakes are not only unobtrusive but durable too; and unlike twine, they won't snap under the pressure of plant growth at the height of summer. In such a closed canopy, most weed growth is suppressed, but some fungal diseases can be troublesome and mildew will need attention in dry seasons. Aphids should be expected on young shoots, so a combined insecticide and fungicide, such as those used on roses, will help to check pests and diseases.

Bedding plants and annuals

Annuals can be used in two main ways: as standby plants to fill in gaps in more permanent plantings or to create features in their own right. In the former role, such types as lobelia, impatiens and white alyssum are very valuable at the front of the mixed border while taller growing plants like nicotianas, African marigolds, salvias and even pelargoniums can be used further back. The rapid growth of most annuals makes them particularly useful in these situations. But the bed more or less confined to annual bedding plants is a very different and rather special feature, dear to the hearts of many gardeners, especially those with smaller gardens and no room for massed borders.

It must be accepted that the annual border *is* an annual feature, a glory for the summer but empty at other times unless it contains biennials, such as wallflowers or sweet Williams, or bulbs used for out-of-season effect, planted in the fall and lifted in the spring. The great merits of annual bedding plants as a group are that they are easy to raise, easy to grow, produce an immense amount of color in a huge range of shades, require no long-term planning and care, being discarded to the compost pile after the summer is spent, and need a minimal amount of soil preparation. Against this must be set the time-consuming consequences of growing very quickly on shallow root systems – they will need regular watering and feeding with liquid fertilizer. But what a small price to pay for some of the loveliest little garden plants.

The annual bed is almost always planned as a fairly formal entity, for while mixed and irregular groupings of different types can be made, this is very difficult to achieve satisfactorily. A degree of formal arrangement in planting is part of the appeal of annuals, providing a welcome contrast to the planned informality of the mixed border. The generally much more restricted height range among annuals (sunflowers being a dramatic exception) also mitigates against mimicking the border plantings.

It is perfectly possible to sow annuals directly into their flowering positions, but this is rarely the best technique. Many annuals will be unable to put on sufficient growth if you hold back from sowing until the end of May while the irregular germination of any seeds sown outdoors makes the likelihood of unsightly gaps appearing in the bed very high. On the whole it is preferable to use plants for almost all annual flowers, either raised yourself indoors from seed or bought as transplants in the spring.

There are fortunately no rules about the way that you choose the plants for your annual flower bed. The overall effect can be anything from the riot of vivid orange and yellow that you will obtain from the numerous varieties of African and French marigolds, the red, white and blue or other patriotic symbolism of the likes of alyssum, lobelia and salvia, or the subtle silver and gray foliage plants like cineraria in combination with selections of white pelargoniums, petunias and nicotianas. Nor are there rules about the arrangement of the plants, which can be a simple alternation of colors or a really dramatic and visually arresting pattern like the so-called carpet bedding, beloved of the Victorians and still to be seen in some public parks.

Whether you raise your own summer bedding plants or buy them, don't try to be too economical. There is always the possibility that a few plants will fail to establish or succumb to some pest or disease attack. Gaps in a formal planting can look unsightly, so always keep a few in reserve for filling in at a later stage.

Annuals are probably the most versatile of all types of garden flower. They are available in a huge range of varieties, and can be grown in almost any situation and in a garden of any size. Grow mixtures of annuals or use them in combination with hardy perennials or even

shrubs, if you wish. To maintain an attractive show right through the summer, such as the petunias (far left) or pelargoniums and lobelias (left) and busy Lizzies (above), featured here, you must feed regularly with a liquid fertilizer. You must also remove dead heads regularly, almost the only exceptions being those plants like lobelia that have flowers too small to be handled individually.

Shrubs

Imagine garden plants that last for years, offer a huge range of size and shape, of leaf form and color, flower color, flower size and flowering season, the possibilities of perfume and the ability to suppress weeds, and yet require minimal attention. It sounds too good to be true; every gardener's idea of Utopia. Yet the world of shrubs offers you all of these options and more besides. I know gardens containing nothing except shrubs and lawns and yet there is never a day of the year on which they don't offer some interest. Of course, to achieve this degree of continuity, a fairly large number of shrubs and a fairly large area is necess-

ary, but every garden will benefit from having at least some shrubs.

There are three main ways in which you can use shrubs in your garden: in a mixed border with herbaceous perennials and other plants; in a dedicated shrubbery, where a blend of different types is grown, usually to the exclusion of other types of plant except possibly bulbs, or dotted around the garden as individual specimens. In the smaller garden, the latter option is the best and a well-chosen shrub can, for instance, form the focal point, help to lead the eye to some particular part of the garden or be used to hide an unsightly feature. But there are impor-

tant aspects to consider as you browse through the shrub section at your garden supply store and find yourself bewildered by the range of types on offer.

Evergreen shrubs provide year-round greenery and the best permanent screening, although for purely visual interest, deciduous types with attractive bark or buds can be as successful. For optimum ground cover, choose prostrate or very slightly arching forms but remember that unless they too are evergreen, early season weed growth will still come through. If space is limited, it is usually best to choose a plant that is naturally fairly

Shrubs like this broom (left) provide an extremely effective and decorative framework around which to plant a mixed border. The hydrangea and fuchsia (below) intermingle attractively to provide a permanent feature that gives color and variety alongside a path or yard, while small specimen shrubs such as the charming dwarf willow, Salix lanata (right), can play a valuable role throughout the seasons even in a small garden.

low growing rather than face the annual pruning back of a vigorous one that will very soon lose its shape. In general, a shrub that has compelling flowers usually has less interesting foliage and so in a small garden with room for very few shrubs, it may be wiser to suppress your enthusiasm for a particularly attractive bloom, concede that it will only color your garden for a few weeks of the year, and opt instead for an appealing leaf form and color or attractive stems.

Most shrubs demand minimal attention, but you must give them the best possible start by buying good quality plants, avoiding cut-price offers (especially those sometimes made by mail order from non-specialist nurseries) and by planting them with due care to their growing conditions. Thereafter, provide an early season application of a balanced fertilizer, just after the first freeze of the fall, and a thick mulch to help moisture retention around the roots; and you will be richly rewarded.

Gardeners tend to think of shrubs as permanent occupants of their garden borders, but in fact most shrubs are fairly slow growing. Even if you are prepared to pay extra for a good sized plant it will take time to reach its full size. If you plant your shrubs at their ideal spacings in a shrubbery, there will be large gaps of bare earth between for many years. A good solution to the problem is to fill in with herbaceous plants and be prepared to remove them as their neighbors grow.

There is probably nowhere in the garden where the vertical layers of plant growth are more apparent or significant than in the shrubbery. Because of this, it is important to check not only the ultimate height but also the relative shade tolerance of your purchases, for while some shrubs will be happy reaching up for the light, others need the protection and comparative shade that their larger companions provide.

Roses

A garden without roses is like chocolate cake without the chocolate. Indisputably it is the queen of flowers but it is more than that, for to talk of *the* rose as if it was but one plant is to mislead to an alarming extent. A modern, almost continuously blooming orangeade-colored floribunda is as far removed from an old-fashioned shell-pink flowered and heavily scented climbing Bourbon as a camellia is from a cabbage. Yet rose they both are and assuredly among their kin there must be a plant to suit every taste.

The first thing is to ignore anyone who tells you that roses are for heavy clay soils only. Certainly they grow well in such conditions but they grow well in any fertile moisture retentive soil and even a light and undernourished sandy loam can be improved by digging in compost or manure and using fertilizer.

But which of the many types of rose should you select and how should you use them in the garden? It is easiest to think of roses in three main groups — modern bush roses, old shrub roses and climbers.

Modern bush roses

The modern bush roses make up the vast majority of non-climbing roses in gardens. They are divided into large flowered roses or hybrid teas and cluster flowered roses or floribundas. The former generally have fairly large and sometimes scented flowers borne singly on their stems while the latter have clusters of blooms, usually smaller and less scented. Both are available in a wide range of colors from white to oranges, pinks and reds. They range from about one to six feet in height but all need pruning annually if they are to give of their best. Almost all bloom on and off throughout the summer, giving a continuity of flowers. In northern gardens, the base of the rose should be protected in winter with a mound of light, well-drained mulch.

The scope offered to a gardener by roses is vast and it is sad when those who dislike the conventional monoculture, as seen in a bed of modern bush roses, dismiss the entire family and overlook the other options. It is scarcely credible, for instance, that the glorious hybrid tea Peace (top), the moss rose James Veitch (above) and the floribunda Iceberg (left) all belong to the same genus. And the possible variations in planting plans are also vast, ranging from the cottage-type garden mixture with pinks (top left) to the exquisite blend of two climbing varieties with a clematis (far left).

PRUNING ROSES

When pruning any type of rose always make the cut sloping away from an outward facing bud.

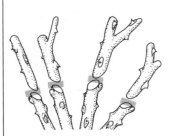

With hybrid teas, cut out any dead, diseased or crossing over shoots in spring (top) and cut back all of the remainder by at least half (center) – rather more for a weak growing variety and rather less for a strong one. Tip back all shoots in fall to minimize damage by winter wind (bottom).

With floribundas, you should aim to take out one-third of the old wood each year in spring by cutting back to the base (top) and cut back each of the remaining shoots by one-third (center). Any dead or diseased wood must also be cut out. Tip back all of the flowering shoots and any very long stems at the end of flowering (bottom).

HYBRID TEA

FLORIBUNDA

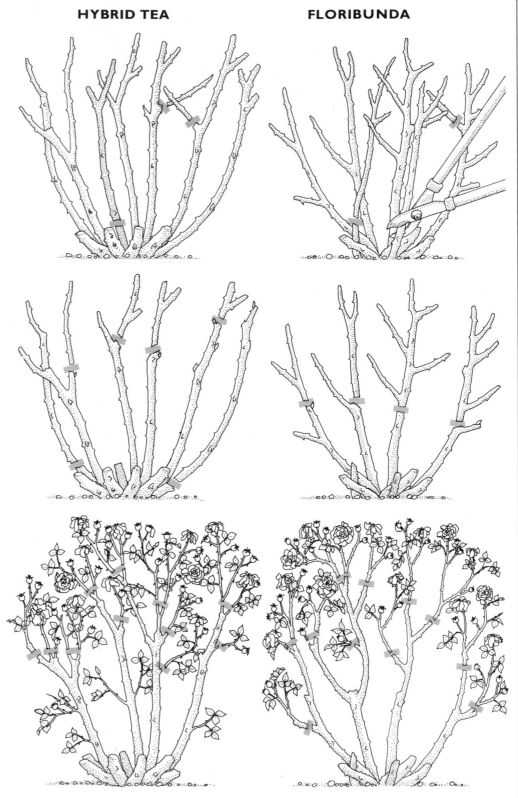

Shrub roses

Old shrub roses are very different from the modern bush roses. They are called old because most varieties originated before the present century and some actually go back as far as the Middle Ages. Like other ornamental shrubs, they are allowed to attain their natural size instead of being restricted by pruning. Their flowers are usually either white or glorious shades of red and pink. They are often tall plants — eight or ten feet is not unusual – but the owner of a small garden should not be put off by this for there are some small and compact types too.

Unlike bush roses but like other shrubs, they need the minimum of pruning; little more than a tidying up. Although most shrub roses are old varieties, there are a few excellent modern shrub roses too. But they all differ from modern bush roses in their much more limited flowering season. Many bloom once, but magnificently, in June only; others have a second, usually sparser, blooming later in the summer, and by choosing your varieties carefully it is possible to have at least some shrub roses in flower from early summer until late fall. Many roses are subject to a number of foliar disease problems. To avoid regular spraying with fungicides, choose disease resistant varieties.

There are other virtues to the old shrub roses, including the pleasant fact that they require very little pruning apart from an annual removal of dead or very old wood. Many of them also produce very attractive and colorful hips which keep up their interest after the flowers have faded. Some, especially those in the Rugosa group, also have delightful fall foliage colors, thus providing even greater value.

In milder areas, many rose varieties can be bought as standards. Prune the heads as though they were bushes.

SHRUB ROSES

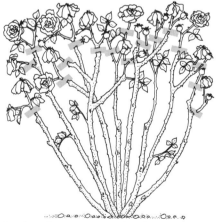

1 In spring, cut out any dead or diseased shoots, cut back about one-third of other long shoots by half and tip back any damaged by frost.

2 After flowering, tip back any very long, whippy growths but leave the flowering heads on those varieties that bear attractive hips.

Climbers

The climbing roses are perhaps the most motley assortment of all for almost all groups of roses include at least a few climbing forms. So there are climbing modern large and cluster flowered roses just as there are climbing old roses of various types. The flowering time of a climber generally reflects that of the group to which it belongs. So the climbing versions of modern roses usually bloom for a long time, while those of old roses do not. And the pruning of modern climbers needs a little more care and attention than does that of old ones.

There is one particular group of climbing roses, however, that has no counterpart among bush and shrub types. The delightfully sprawling rambler roses are the roses of picture postcard cottages. Many have truly beautiful blooms and divine perfume but they have two big drawbacks; almost all bloom in early summer only and require a careful annual pruning that may seem akin to butchery.

Vigor is another important point to consider with climbing roses, for the strongest growing climbers are plants of phenomenal prowess, capable of reaching 45 feet or more and of producing individual shoots 20 feet long in a single season. These are clearly not plants for any but the very largest gardens, although at the other end of the spectrum there are the slow growing climbers that are sometimes called pillar roses because they can be trained against a large pillar or post and take several years even to attain six feet.

Miniatures

Finally, there come the miniatures, a group of exquisite little roses, barely 16in tall. These are undemanding, amenable to being grown in pots or around terraces, as edging to beds or almost anywhere you care to pop them in. Treat them, as you should treat all roses, to a twice yearly dressing of rose

fertilizer (once as growth starts in spring and again after the summer flowering), and they will grace your garden for year after year.

Gardeners often ask whether there are any plants that they can grow beneath the roses in a rose bed — something to cover up the unsightly bare earth when the roses are not in bloom. The problem with this is that any plants beneath will interfere with some operation in rose care — feeding or mulching especially. If you object to bare earth, you might prefer to grow your roses with other shrubs and perennials in a mixed border.

It is often overlooked that some of the old shrub roses, like Rosa rugosa Alba *(top), have more than one attractive feature: once the early summer blooms have passed, there is the prospect of lovely fall hips to look forward to.*

Although rambler roses, like Albertine (above), flower rather briefly in early summer and require thorough pruning if they are to give of their best, they offer ample reward in a combination of glorious bloom and enchanting perfume.

CLIMBERS AND RAMBLERS

There are three main groups of roses here. Group 1 (top) comprises the true ramblers; roses like Dorothy Perkins, American Pillar, Crimson Showers and François Juranville. Group 2 (middle) includes most of the other popular ramblers like Albéric Barbier, Albertine, New Dawn, Paul's Scarlet Climber and The Garland. Almost all other rambling and climbing roses, including all of the climbing sports of hybrid teas and floribundas, belong to Group 3 (bottom).

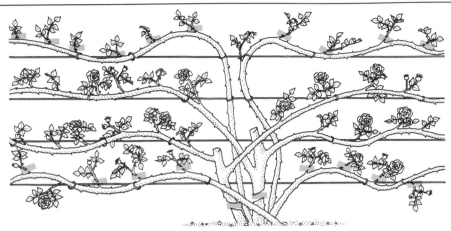

Group 1. Cut back almost all of the flowered shoots to the base at the end of flowering but leave a few to retain a framework. Cut back the laterals on these to two or three buds from the base.

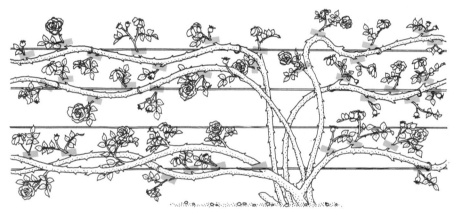

Group 2. After flowering, cut back two or three of the oldest shoots to the base and remove any diseased or damaged wood. Tie in all other shoots and shorten their laterals to two or three buds from the base.

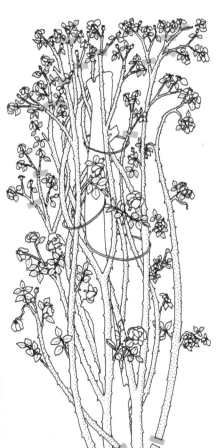

Pillar roses are upright shrubs or slow growing climbers trained onto a pillar. Prune them very lightly.

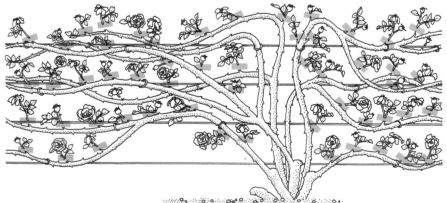

Group 3. Between the end of flowering and spring, cut back all of the flowered laterals to two or three buds, cut out any very old shoots and prune and retrain new long growths to replace them.

Climbing plants

Climbing plants are not inherently any different from their free-standing relations except that their stems are too weak to support them. When choosing climbers for your garden, therefore, many of the criteria are the same as those when choosing shrubs – when do they flower, are they deciduous or evergreen, how hardy are they, how much care and attention do they need?

The only important additional question to be answered is whether or not the plant is self-clinging, for self-clinging climbers like English ivy or Virginia creeper will so tightly embrace a wall as to need no help in the form of wires or trellis. This saves the need for a support, but clinging ivy can damage old brickwork and crumbling mortar, and clinging evergreens can cause damp to accumulate. Against a house wall, it is much safer to choose a non-clinging, preferably deciduous climber, using rustless bolts so the

trellis can be freed when you want to decorate.

Climbers provide an invaluable vertical dimension and there is a place for them in every garden; in fact, I view bare house walls and bare fences in much the same way as expanses of bare soil – as wasted growing space. Provided you choose a plant with growth vigor commensurate with the space available, you can select from climbing roses, clematis, ivies, honeysuckle, parthenocissus vines, or even annual climbers such as morning glory if you don't object to the wall being uncovered in winter. One precaution is to read the label carefully and don't plant a climber like the rose Kiftsgate, that can put on 16ft in a season, against a wall only 13ft tall.

Any established garden is almost certain to contain sizable trees, and just as climbers in the wild are most often to be found growing up trees, so they

can be used to ornament the trees in your garden. No established tree with a stem more than about 2in in diameter will be harmed by having a climber wrapped around it, and by choosing your rose, clematis or other climber carefully, you can embellish the tree in one of two ways. Choose a climber that flowers at the same time as an ornamental tree to produce a delightful complement of colors or alternatively choose one that flowers at a different time of year to lengthen the overall period of interest.

The third and possibly most interesting way of all to use climbers is to grow them on vertical frameworks where none existed before. Archways bedecked with roses or honeysuckle can be used to provide partial divisions between different areas of the garden, while arbors, sometimes known as pergolas, give shade and a pleasant environment in which you can sit.

A wall or fence will reflect heat and enhance the temperature close by, which makes it possible to grow climbers or wall shrubs (plants like pyracanthas that do not actually climb but can be trained against a wall) that would be too tender elsewhere in the garden. On the other hand, the soil at the base of a wall or fence is not only warm but dry too and any climbing plant will need special attention to its watering needs if it is to give of its best. As a result, it is essential to incorporate organic material thoroughly into the soil before planting and to use an organic mulch later.

While some climbing plants require rather careful training if they are to appear at their most attractive, others are better allowed a freer rein. Honeysuckles (left) or some types of clematis (right) should be planted where they have sufficient room to cascade and tumble in living evocation of the cottager's world.

WALL SUPPORTS

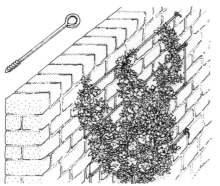

Eyes are hard metal pegs with a hole at one end. Hammered into mortar, they are used for attaching training wires. Eyed screws driven into wooden pegs are an alternative.

Lead-headed nails are useful for training climbers with a few, widely and irregularly placed shoots but have the disadvantage that the plant is attached very closely.

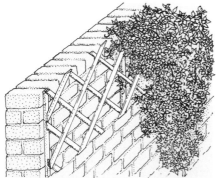

Trellis has the merit of remaining attractive even when deciduous climbers are reduced to bare stems in the winter. Attach trellises or frames to treated battens.

Troughs and hollow walls

Among the most admired features of our great horticultural meccas are their rock gardens, where every plant personifies neatness and aesthetic satisfaction scaled down to apparently manageable proportions. Sadly, a rock garden is one of the most laborious and expensive garden features to build if it is to take on any semblance of being natural (and a poorly constructed and inappropriately sited rock garden looks ludicrous). Fortunately, this does not mean that most of us should ignore rock plants – the solution is to grow your alpine plants in a trough or hollow wall instead of in a traditional rock garden.

A trough, in its ideal form, is an old cattle or horse trough, hollowed out from a block of granite or durable gritstone. This is now almost prohibitively expensive and a modern reconstituted stone substitute suffices for many gardeners. Cheaper still and not too difficult to make is a trough that consists of an old glazed sink covered with a home-made, peat-and-cement concoction generally called hypertufa. This will give a remarkably good semblance of the real thing and the appearance can be enhanced further by painting the whole with either milk or liquid manure – or even both, if you can tolerate the aroma. This will encourage the growth of moss, algae and lichens and is a useful technique for ageing any fresh stone or concrete.

The main requirement for a trough or a hollow wall garden is good drainage. An old sink should, of course, already have a suitable drainage hole and a genuine trough can be drilled by a stonemason, but if you are constructing a hollow wall, ensure that some gaps are left in the sides, especially toward the base, if the stone or bricks are mortared. There are no hard and fast rules regarding the ideal dimensions for a trough or hollow wall garden, although a hollow wall less than about 6in wide really is rather too

AGEING A TROUGH

An old glazed sink or other durable modern container can be given a treatment to render it similar to an authentic (but much more costly) stone trough.

Cover the whole with a mixture called hypertufa – one part by volume cement, one part sharp sand and two parts moss peat made into a thick, porridge-like mixture.

restricting – it will scarcely allow you sufficient individual plants to offer continuity of color and interest.

The importance of good drainage should be reflected in the potting mix used within the trough or hollow wall. The ideal blend is a mixture of three parts of a soil-based brand-name potting mix with one part of horticultural grit. Again for the sake of drainage, make sure if you are constructing a hollow wall that it is not laid on top of a very solid base of garden soil – always fork the surface in the base of the wall thoroughly and preferably lay broken bricks or crocks to improve the drainage still further.

Within the trough or hollow wall you can grow almost any plants that are not too tall, too rapidly and widely spreading or too invasive. Perhaps the popular alpines like dwarf potentillas, mossy and other saxifrages, the smaller thymes, some of the sedums like

Sedum spathulifolium, small primulas and Campanula cochlearifolia best exemplify these characteristics. A specialist alpine nursery or good garden supply store should be able to help you with knowledgeable advice, and it is well worth asking before you buy, for there are species of campanula, dwarf phlox and sedum that can rapidly overgrow a restricted garden of this type. A trough or hollow wall garden is also an ideal environment for some of the miniature conifers but, once again, be advised by your supplier, for while some, like Juniperus communis var. compressa, are very slow growing and remain small and compact, others do not stay dwarf for long.

If your hollow wall is large enough, it is possible to grow more vigorous, spreading and arching dwarf shrubs, such as Cotoneaster dameri, winter jasmine (Jasminum nudiflorum) or Juniperus horizontalis Blue Rug.

There are two main ways in which you can use a trough or hollow wall garden. The traditional way is to make a permanent planting of alpines such as gentians (left) – a very much simpler way of growing these delightful species than in a full-sized rock garden. Alternatively, use bedding plants much as you would in window boxes or other types of container. And who can deny that a hollow wall, brimming with lobelia, ivy leaved pelargoniums and petunias (above), makes a welcoming feature as visitors approach your front gate?

Plants for containers

There is almost no limit to the range of plant types that can be grown in containers, the only constraint being that big, tree-sized plants require big pots. With this proviso, it is perfectly possible to grow small trees, especially fruit trees on dwarfing rootstocks, in a container of half-barrel size, about 24in in diameter. In fact, in a small or very small garden a container may offer you the only way in which trees can be grown at all, but even in much larger gardens, containers of shrubs both large and tiny can be used to provide an additional, portable dimension to the garden environment.

The standard practice with containers is to fill them with bulbs in the early part of the year and then lift these and replace them with half-hardy summer flowering plants as soon as the danger of frost is past. This is fine, but among the stylish and more unusual plants that can be grown in containers are climbers such as clematis, English ivy, or even annual types such as sweet peas. Placed in containers, they will trail delightfully over the sides rather than climb, an effect that is particularly striking if the container is placed on top of a bank. Even the climbing vegetables like pole beans and peas can be grown in this way, or you can grow a fruit tree, such as an apple on a dwarfing rootstock (though unless you choose a family apple tree, you will need two for pollination). There is indeed enormous scope for your own inventiveness in the planting of containers, provided always that you fertilize and water the plants much more frequently than you would in the open garden.

The only real restriction on plants for containers is that they should not be so vigorous as to outgrow their space. Planting can be simple with one or two species only (top right) or more complex (right and far right), but remember that the keys to success are water and fertilizer.

Bulbs

Mention bulbs and you will probably conjure up a vision of the massed daffodils and tulips to be seen in public parks and gardens. Although these understandably and perhaps justifiably account for the vast majority of the bulbs bought and planted each year, they are really only the tip of a very large iceberg. Given a little thought and planning, it would be possible to provide year-round garden color using bulbs, corms and tubers alone. This may be an extreme view, but it pays rich visual dividends if you are adventurous both in the range of bulbs that you buy and in the way that you use them in the garden.

Almost all garden bulbs (using the term in its popular sense to include corms and similar structures) are long-term garden investments. With the common exceptions of the St Brigid or de Caen types of *Anemone coronaria* (in most gardens at least) and perhaps some of the dwarf spring flowering irises, like *Iris danfordiae*, all bulbs will last for several seasons and give you a very good return for your investment; many, indeed, will naturalize, spread and become more or less permanent. Never skimp on quality, therefore, when buying new stock.

Daffodils and narcissi are immensely popular, so perhaps it is inevitable that they should sometimes be used unwisely or to excess. A good rule is to avoid the temptation to buy them in mixtures of several varieties. The overall impact is diminished, not enhanced, by having relatively few in flower at any one time, and the appearance of the later flowering types will be greatly lessened by their being surrounded by the dead flower heads of the earlier varieties. This ugliness can easily be avoided by planting in discrete groups of about ten or twelve bulbs of each variety, using the information given on the pack label for relative flowering times.

Daffodils look particularly attractive

when grown in grass, especially beneath trees, but the choice must be selective, for not all varieties are vigorous enough to compete with the grass; once again, the label should help you – the designation 'good for naturalizing' is a sound guide. Remember that the foliage must remain for at least six weeks after the flowers are finished, and this will interfere with mowing – an important consideration if the plants are in an otherwise manicured lawn. Restricting them to the bases around trees growing within the lawn is often the ideal solution.

The short-trumpeted daffodils known as narcissi look particularly delightful in a border and provide color early in the season before the other border perennials appear. Once again, the foliage is less than attractive after the flowering period is over, so the groups are best arranged where up and coming, large leaved or bushy plants like lupins or phlox will gradually conceal them.

Daffodils and narcissi are also good subjects for large containers and, by planting them in discrete layers, continuity of flowering can be achieved. The drawback is that after flowering you will have a container of foliage for a period before the bulbs can be lifted and the containers replanted.

Large numbers of the familiar large flowered hybrid tulips can cause problems, especially in a small garden. Their foliage is unattractive after flowering, they must be allowed time to die down and they need additional garden space if they are lifted and heeled in elsewhere for this to occur. A good solution in this case might be to use small and discrete groups of a few choice large flowered varieties and concentrate your tulip plantings instead on the many smaller flowered species now becoming freely available. These need not be lifted each year; they have much less unsightly foliage and will naturalize and spread very effectively.

Lilies (far left) make excellent container plants. Keep some in a greenhouse in the early part of the spring to advance their flowering time. Irises (left) are invaluable in the mixed border and, provided they are planted at a shallow depth, will multiply easily on most soils. The best gladioli to grow are the butterfly varieties (above) which have smaller, less assertive flower spikes.

There are several other valuable bulbous border plants. Gladioli are effective when used in small groups but suffer the disadvantage that, not being hardy, they must be lifted and replanted each year. Perhaps a better way to use them is quite separately from other flowers, close to the house and the kitchen garden, where they can be cut for arrangement indoors.

Dahlias, too, are not hardy and can be very assertive when massed. Try using twos and threes of the medium flowered cactus and decorative types with the very neat pom-pom forms in the border – but remember that the need to lift large numbers of dahlias from a mixed border every fall can cause a great deal of disturbance to the permanent, hardy inhabitants.

Less commonly seen in the border but very useful in small groups are ornamental alliums, relatives of the onion. Imagine the lovely flowers of chives but much larger and on stems up to five feet tall and you will appreciate how striking these plants can be for the back of the border – and for flower arranging.

Many lily species and varieties naturalize well in the garden and provide stunning and unexpected bloom as they emerge unobtrusively from amongst other, more common, border plants. The taller and more reliable types, like the regal lily (*Lilium regale*), are a comparatively trouble-free option. Also worth considering are the unrelated day lilies, *Hemerocallis,* that are now available in a wide variety of colors and that spread easily and quickly.

The large flowered bearded irises bring splendid early summer color to the border – the intermediate types are more robust than the slightly later flowering tall forms and seldom need staking. Most gardens have the blues and purples but the rich orange-browns provide an elegant touch of class.

The varieties and species of dwarf bulbs are legion. For growing in grass, nothing betters crocus, but use the large flowered Dutch types for this purpose and plant them in drifts — oranges on the one hand and a mixture of purple and white on the other. The many other types of smaller flowered crocus like varieties of the admirable *Crocus chrysanthus* and *C. sieberi* are best kept for the trough and hollow wall gardens. Plant separate groups of ten to fifteen corms to give splashes of early season color. They can be followed by *Anemone blanda* and the smaller flowered tulip species such as *T. pulchella*, *T. biflora* and *T.*

urumiensis. Use the more striking red flowered forms of *T. praestans* and *T. griegii* as complements to white flowered spring shrubs and blossom trees, planting groups beneath white cherries or magnolias for stunning contrasts. Hardy species of cyclamen provide invaluable groundcover in difficult situations beneath trees. Some of the species now offered are expensive, barely hardy and difficult to grow, but if you concentrate on *C. hederifolium* and *C. coum*, you should have no problems. In an area where grass can easily be left unmown, the snake's head fritillary, with its subtle patterning, makes a splendid choice.

Dahlias (far left) are not everyone's choice, but a range of the smaller flowered forms integrate well with each other, while hybrid tulips (left) are now available in almost bewildering variety. Among daffodils, start your spring with the tiny hoop petticoat, Narcissus bulbocodium *(top), which appears well before the familiar large flowered Dutch crocuses (above).*

Trees

Other than on the very smallest, inner city site, a garden without trees is, for me, unthinkable. On the other hand there are few areas of gardening in which so many mistakes are made, so painfully and so expensively. When it comes to choosing such a large and long-lasting feature, it pays to give the matter considerable thought, choosing the right species and the best place.

Forest trees, like oaks, beech and linden, are, by and large, for forests. They will rapidly cast shade over most of your garden; possibly damage the foundations of your house, and deplete the soil of moisture and nutrient over a large area. Far better for gardens are trees of limited ultimate height and spread that offer some special feature of appealing foliage, bark or flowers. You will see selections of crab apples, flowering cherries, small Asian maple species and many others at nurseries or your local garden supply stores. Check their ultimate height and always keep this in mind when planting near your house. Some trees such as magnolias and many fruit trees can be grown against a wall but do seek advice first.

When you are planting a tree or trees, use them to serve a purpose in addition to their intrinsic aesthetic appeal. A tree, for instance, makes a good focal point in a planting design, and it can be used to screen an eyesore or to cast some cooling shade over the house and patio. Work out in your mind's eye where a tree, when it has reached its full span and height, will throw shade at different times of day.

A tree alone, no matter how attractive, can be stark, so try to create a small habitat and environment around it. Underplant it with bulbs or with shade tolerant ground covers. Because competition from other plants can slow a tree's growth, underplanting may be delayed until the tree is established. And remember that a seat beneath a small attractive tree always provides a pleasant place to sit in summer.

Trees are essential for all except the very tiniest gardens, but choose carefully or they will outgrow their welcome. Their appeal can take many forms – witness the blossom of a cherry (above), blending with the naturalized daffodils, the foliage of a variegated dogwood (right) or the fiery fall colors of a Japanese maple (left).

Part 5

FOOD FROM YOUR GARDEN

For many gardeners, the real hallmark of their gardening success is not that their garden looks attractive and is admired by all-comers but that they can dine on the results of their labors. Certainly, for reasons that are largely inexplicable, but may be as much psychological as real, fruits and vegetables picked fresh from one's own garden usually taste better than those bought at the supermarket. No special or unique skills are attached to growing food plants, although each type of fruit and vegetable crop has its own particular demands. I cannot believe that most beginners in gardening want immediately to plunge in at the deep end and expect to provide full self-sufficiency for the family; nor that many will ever want to grow the least interesting crops or those that are relatively cheap to buy. Accordingly, this section takes what I call the expanded kitchen garden approach and gives selective guidance on the most reward-ing, interesting, toothsome and easily grown fruit and vegetable crops for a fairly small area – the crops, in fact, that give me the greatest gardening satisfaction.

Perhaps the most important aspect of growing plants to eat rather than just to look at is that a little extra care and attention to fertilizing, watering and weeding is needed. A somewhat neglected bed of roses or tub of bedding plants will still give you an acceptably attractive display, but you will find very little to eat in a kitchen garden that has only been accorded modest attention for more than a year or so. So weeding and feeding are called for, but, on the other hand, you will largely be spared concern with pests and diseases, for in general it is unwise to spray your food crops with chemical pesticides and I think you should be prepared for the possibility of having to share at least a little of your produce with other members of the animal kingdom.

The main reason for growing fruit and vegetables is, of course, as food, but planted carefully and integrated with flowers, they can be used to create visually attractive gardens.

Planning a kitchen garden

When you plan and plant an ornamental garden, the considerations governing where each plant should be placed are largely aesthetic. In the case of fruit and vegetables, however, there is a little more to take into account. It has already been pointed out that to produce anything worth eating, a crop plant needs some extra attention in terms of its own feeding. For we place very great demands on our food plants – think of the difference between a wild vetch growing in the hedgerow and its relative, the garden pea, with wonderfully swollen and succulent pods, and you will gain some idea of the difference. Continually pumping more and more fertilizer into the soil is one way of achieving this improvement, and this is largely the method that modern commercial farming has adopted, growing the same type of crop on the same land for year after year.

In our vegetable gardens, we can be more civilized and much kinder to the environment by ensuring that all plants are given the opportunity to use the

In this simplified rotation plan, the numbers of plants shown do not represent the actual numbers to be grown. By identifying the crops on the first year plan, you will be able to see how they are moved in the second and third years. Reading from left to right in the first year, therefore, are: (top row) carrots and beets, spinach and Swiss chard, lettuces, early potatoes, bush beans, peppers (start under cloches), bush tomatoes, radishes and green onions, trailing cucumbers, pole beans; (bottom row) carrots and beets, broccoli, rhubarb and herbs, peas protected with wire netting, corn, trailing squashes and pole beans. The pole beans, herbs and rhubarb aren't moved each year. The total dimensions of the plot are 33ft by 46ft.

CROP ROTATION

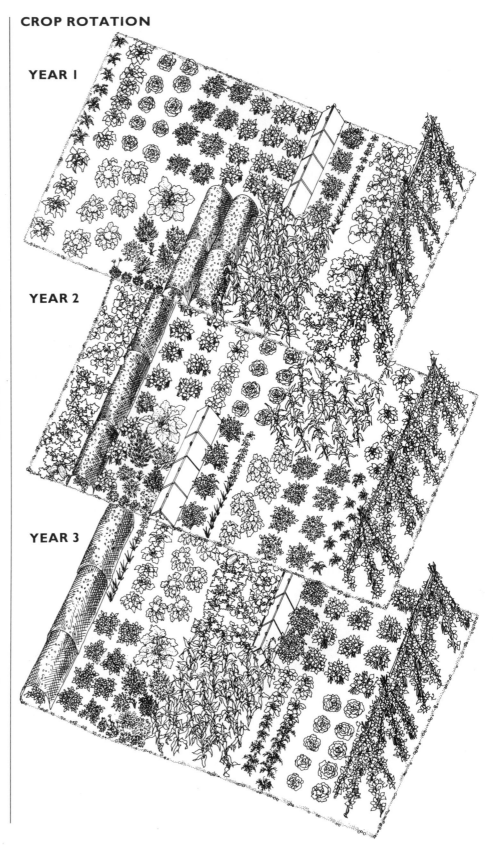

YEAR 1

YEAR 2

YEAR 3

soil's food reserves to the full, so that we can keep to a minimum the amount of fertilizer that we need to add. This is achieved by the expedient of crop rotation, which is nothing more complex than ensuring that the same types of vegetable are not grown on exactly the same area of soil for more than one year in three.

For the purposes of a rotation, vegetable crops are divided into three main groups which reflect their fertilizer or nutritional needs – first, root crops like carrots, parsnips and potatoes; second, peas and beans; and third, leafy vegetables like cabbages, cauliflowers and Brussels sprouts. The vegetable garden as a whole is divided into three equal areas, on each of which the three groups are changed or rotated each season. Salad vegetables and other minor or very quick growing crops are slotted into the plan where and when this is convenient.

All of this theory and practice works best in a full-sized vegetable garden where almost all types of crop are being grown. In the smaller scale kitchen garden that concerns me here, there are few potatoes and even fewer of the large leafy vegetables, but disproportionate amounts of beans and salad crops. This makes full crop rotation impossible, but the plan suggested here offers a reasonable compromise. This plan goes a considerable way toward ensuring that all plants will have their fair share of the nutrients already available in the soil, though it

Almost no garden is so small that its owner can't savor at least a little home-grown produce. Those few lettuces and herbs (top) that you have grown will always taste better than any you buy from a store, and rather than trying to become self-sufficient from too small an area, it is better to grow a little of most things (left) to provide an interesting variety of vegetables.

will still be necessary to supplement with some form of fertilizer. Crop rotation is also important because it helps to slow the build-up of soil-borne insects and diseases.

A glance at the plan will indicate that there are some vegetables that must stay in the same place for year after year – either because, like rhubarb, they are perennials rather than annuals or because, like pole beans, they have particular site requirements. The herb garden, too, usually stays in one place. It will also be apparent that there are a few vegetables that always need some form of protection around them, either in the shape of cloches or a greenhouse.

But I hope that you won't think of the kitchen garden as a purely functional place. Talk of rotations and fertilizers tends to obscure the fact that the vegetable, salad and herb garden is an attractive garden feature in its own right. The brilliant crimson stalks of rhubarb chard, for example, are an eye-catcher in any vegetable garden. These are attractive from early summer until the first hard freeze of fall. Edge the vegetable beds with parsley or chives and even intersperse some flowering ornamentals (low growing varieties of old shrub roses look magnificent among herbs) to create something that is uniquely attractive and good to eat.

When you come to the fruit garden, rather different planning considerations apply. With the exception of strawberries, fruit are distinctly longer term propositions than vegetables – bush and cane fruit should give at least seven years' service and tree fruit, of course, very much longer. As a result, there is no scope for rotation and the important considerations are very much those of choosing a good, sunny site, preparing the ground thoroughly before planting, buying the best possible planting stock and using the available area to the full by growing sufficient of each type of fruit without inflicting a glut of any on the household. By training fruit plants in certain ways, it is possible further to optimize the use of a particular growing area.

In addition, bush and cane fruits, strawberries and cherries also need protection from birds, which in some areas will rapidly strip any crop as it ripens. Some form of netting cover is almost essential, and a fruit cage makes a sound and worthwhile investment. This may be either a bought or purpose-made lightweight aluminum structure or a framework of wooden posts and chicken wire such as most reasonably handy gardeners could construct themselves.

Avoid over-planting – one dwarf apple tree (above left) and one clump of rhubarb (above) will be adequate for most families, while those who find vegetable and fruit gardens unattractive can integrate them with flowers in the traditional French manner (right).

Tomatoes and peppers

Nothing can beat plump, vine ripened tomatoes for enlivening a summer picnic.

Tomatoes can be grown from seed or plants can be purchased from your local garden supply store. If space is available, grow several varieties to suit your palette. Varieties have different ripening times, so it is a good idea to choose one early bearing variety and at least one later selection to extend the season. In northern areas with a short growing season, it is best to stick with the early bearing varieties. Also, give preference to varieties that are leased as disease and nematode resistant, particularly if tomatoes have previously been grown on the site.

When growing tomatoes from seed, sow the seed indoors six to seven weeks before the frost free date in the spring. A sterile brand-name potting mix is the best growing media. Tomatoes have a high light requirement, so

the seedlings must be grown on a bright south-facing window sill or in a sunny greenhouse or cold frame. Sow seed thinly in seed flats and prick out the seedlings to 3in pots after they have formed their first true leaves. The plants should then remain in these pots until they are planted out when the danger of frost has past. To get a jump on the season, some plants could be set out a few weeks earlier if cloches are used to warm and protect them. As with all seedlings grown indoors, it is important to acclimatize them to the outdoors by hardening them off before planting out.

Tomatoes will grow best if they are transplanted into warm soil. When planting, gently tap the plant from its container. Then tease the outer roots away from the rootball so they come into immediate contact with the surrounding soil. Though it is not essential, most tomatoes grow best if staked,

TOMATOES

Planted in a greenhouse soil bed

In a large pot of potting mix

In a bottomless ring on gravel

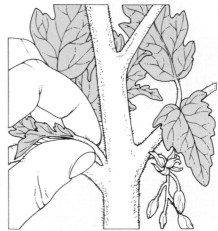

To obtain the maximum crop of good quality fruit, the side shoots that appear adjacent to the leaves can be pinched out to help to create a strong plant. You may need to do this weekly in the early summer.

Most tomatoes have a naturally sprawling habit, like this outdoor bush variety (top left); yet by training you can grow plants in relatively confined spaces (far left). Peppers (left) can be started in the spring under cloches to give them a jump on the season.

especially in moist, humid climates. Use sturdy 6ft stakes and place these before planting the tomatoes to avoid any root damage. As the plants grow, narrow strips of old rags can be used to loosely tie them to the stake. Fertilize at the time of planting with a balanced fertilizer relatively low in nitrogen. Too much nitrogen will cause the plant to produce excessive vegetative growth at the expense of fruit production. Special tomato fertilizers are fine, but these are usually much more expensive than an ordinary farm fertilizer like 5-10-5, which is equally effective. The plants will need daily watering for the initial week after planting. There-

after, only occasional (but thorough) watering during dry periods will be necessary.

Peppers and eggplants

Closely related to tomatoes, peppers and eggplants have very similar growing requirements. They thrive on bright sun and hot weather and are handled just like tomatoes. However, since they mature a bit more slowly than tomatoes, the seed should be sown eight to nine weeks before the frost free date. Unlike tomatoes, eggplants and peppers generally do not need staking.

Most seed catalogs offer a wide selection of pepper varieties. Less culinary diversity is available in eggplants, though they are an important part of any summer harvest. When selecting any vegetable variety, it is a good idea to check with your state cooperative extension agent or local botanic garden for the best selections for your local growing conditions.

Lettuce, spinach and green onions

Lettuce is the most indispensable of salads, spinach perhaps the most under-rated green vegetable and green onions are invaluable, especially to those who are aware that they can be grown almost as a year-round crop. All are very easy to grow in the cool season of spring and fall; all are undemanding but thrive best on a free-draining soil on a plot that has been composted or manured in the previous season (onions are especially appreciative of this), and all can be sown directly into the garden.

Being predominantly leafy crops, lettuces, spinach and onions have a fairly high requirement for nitrogen fertilizer. To cater for this, rake in about 2½oz per square yard of a balanced fertilizer about a week before sowing. Apply the same amount again around and between the plants when they have reached half their full size.

The first secret of growing lettuces successfully is to water them regularly for failure to do this will result in plants with small heads, a bitter taste and a propensity to bolt or run to seed. It is also important to arrange your sowings so that you have a continuous supply and not a glut of heads for a few weeks only.

Begin sowing in early March, in soil pre-warmed for a few days with cloches, and leave the cloches over the early sowings for several weeks more to aid the development of the seedlings. Sow shallowly in rows about 12in apart and make a first thinning as soon as the seedlings are large enough to handle. Thin them to a spacing of about 3in and then, as the plants develop, thin again to a spacing of about 12in with large-headed varieties but only half of this with smaller ones.

To ensure continuity, sow a fresh row or two as the seedlings from the previous sowing emerge. On average, this will take about ten days (rather longer at the start and end of the season, rather less in the middle), so by calculating roughly how much lettuce your family will need every ten days, you can work out how much to sow each time. Make the last spring sowings in late May, using varieties that are heat tolerant or slow to bolt. In August, begin sowing again for fall harvest. Place cloches over these end-of-season plants to help them mature.

If you wish, you can extend the season further by sowing hardier varieties in early fall and leaving them under cloches to mature in late fall. In mild areas, protected lettuce may persist well into the winter. In the greenhouse, you could sow a true winter variety in late summer to be ready for cutting around Christmas time.

It is, naturally, important to choose the right variety for your purpose, and even within the summer-maturing

SEQUENTIAL SOWING

Many gardeners sow all of their lettuces, carrots or other vegetables at the same time, with the result that they also mature at the same time. To avoid this, sow one row of lettuce then sow each further row as the seedlings of the previous one emerge. With other vegetables, choose varieties with different maturing times.

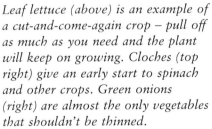

Leaf lettuce (above) is an example of a cut-and-come-again crop – pull off as much as you need and the plant will keep on growing. Cloches (top right) give an early start to spinach and other crops. Green onions (right) are almost the only vegetables that shouldn't be thinned.

crop there are several different types. The butterhead or smooth lettuces have thin, smooth leaves, fairly loosely wrapped together. The crisphead lettuces have crinkly, firmer, crunchy leaves and tend to be larger plants. Cos or romaine lettuces are also fairly crisp but have a markedly upright habit, rather akin to that of Chinese cabbage although they are in no way related to it. Dwarf varieties of all three types are available and are worth considering if your space is limited.

There are two other types: leaf lettuces, typified by the variety Salad Bowl, are not usually cut whole, but used by pulling leaves from the plant as they are needed, while an interesting visual contrast is provided in the salad garden by the so-called red lettuces, that in fact have purplish leaves.

Spinach

Like lettuce, spinach grows quickly, but unlike most lettuce varieties, it is a cut-and-come-again crop. In other words, you pull a small amount from each plant at each picking and then allow more leaves or shoots to develop. If you prefer the traditional 'Popeye' type of spinach, sow at three-week intervals from early March until mid-May. By sowing about 13ft of row (with 12in between rows) each time, you will have sufficient plants to enable you to take ample pickings right through the early summer. Lightly thin the plants to leave about 12 in between them. Like lettuce, spinach will not tolerate mid-summer heat but additional sowings can be started in late August for fall and early winter harvest. Easier than traditional spinach, however, taking up less space overall, more versatile and rather more striking as a plant is Swiss chard. This is a fairly large plant with large leaves and a single row, sown in March and thinned to leave about six plants 16in apart, will be adequate for most family's needs until the fall – or even until well into the winter if you place cloches over them at the end of the summer. The green parts of the leaves are treated like spinach and the thick white midrib can be cooked like asparagus.

Green onions

Growing green onions is absolute simplicity. Sow the seed fairly thinly in rows every four weeks from March until mid-May for a regular supply of plants right through the summer and into the fall. Sow again in September for an early spring crop and again in February, under cloches, to give late spring pulling. Unlike most other vegetables, green onions shouldn't be thinned.

Carrots, beets and radishes

Although they are actually quite unrelated to each other, carrots, beets and radishes belong to the group of vegetables called root crops – for obvious reasons as it is the swollen root that is eaten (although beet tops can in fact be used to make very good soup).

Carrots and radishes have very little demand for fertilizer. One application of a balanced fertilizer applied at the beginning of the season should be sufficient. A soil test will provide information on the application rate needed. No root crops are very tolerant of fresh manure and they should never be sown into soil that has been manured more recently than before the preceding crop. Contact with fresh manure is probably the commonest reason for the roots becoming irregularly shaped or fanged.

As with most vegetables, root crops grow best in a free-draining soil, but carrots are particularly demanding in their soil requirements. It is very difficult to grow carrots in a heavy, wet soil or in any soil that is either shallow or full of stones or hard clods; their roots are simply unable to penetrate adequately and, once again, are likely to be misshapen. In such conditions, try the short or stump rooted types but be prepared for some disappointments. And be prepared too, whenever you grow carrots, for the depredations caused by the root tunneling activities of the maggots of the carrot fly. There is no effective way to control this pest, but as the egg-laying females are attracted by the scent of bruised carrot foliage, it helps if you sow the seed thinly, which lessens the disturbance of the leaves brought about during the thinning operation.

Some gardeners find they can ward off carrot fly attacks by using the fact that the female insects fly fairly close to the ground. By erecting a 'fence' of plastic sheet about 2ft high around the plot, and by keeping the plot as a whole fairly small, it is found that the pests

will fly over the crop and miss it altogether. But whatever else you do, never apply insecticides to the soil when sowing carrots, for more than any other plant they are prone to pick up traces of the chemical, and this will taint the flavor.

Sow seed of early cylindrical rooted varieties very thinly in early March under cloches, in rows about 8in apart, and try to ensure that you have a space of about 2in between seedlings. If you need to thin them, always water the plants thoroughly afterward to deaden the aroma. Sow the same varieties again in early April and then, until mid July, sow every three weeks with a long rooted type. In late summer, sow again with a fast growing cylindrical rooted type, cover with cloches and you should have carrots almost through the winter. Carrots are much tougher than is generally reckoned at withstanding frost when left in the ground and I find this a more reliable way of keeping them than the conventional practice of storing dug roots in boxes of sand.

Beets

Beets have two main problems. They are prone to bolt and they tend to become woody and tasteless. Both conditions can be kept to a minimum if you never allow plants to become too dry, and if you choose the so-called bolt-resisting varieties for the earlier sowings you will find that this helps to avoid, though not eliminate, this annoying habit.

A beet seed is not an individual but a cluster of up to four separate seeds adhering together, so these must be sown thinly (about one inch apart), for up to four seedlings will emerge at each sowing position. Thin the clusters to leave one plant (the strongest seedling) every 2in. The rows should be about 12in apart.

Begin beet sowings with the bolt-resistant globe varieties around the middle of March – cloches may be used

with advantage, especially in cooler, more northerly areas. Like lettuce and spinach, succession planting can be made in the cool seasons to ensure continuous crops. Beets do not grow well, though, in the hottest part of the summer. As the roots swell, make one further thinning to leave a single plant every 4in. Incidentally, cook and enjoy the small, tender young beets that you remove; they are more tender and flavorful than full-grown roots. Pull the remaining roots as they mature but never leave any to swell to more than about 3in in diameter for they then rapidly lose their flavor and become increasingly woody and unpalatable.

Don't over-plant your kitchen garden – with limited space, it is much more interesting and rewarding to try out different types of vegetable and to have one or two rows of several crops (left) rather than to attempt to be self-sufficient in a few. Short rooted carrots (far left top) are ideal on shallower soils. Radishes (far left bottom) offer a wide range of root shape and color, but remember that most types will bolt if sown in mid-summer. Beets (below) are at their most tender when the roots are about golf-ball size.

Beets are not winter hardy and must therefore be lifted and stored for winter use. The best varieties to use for this purpose are not the globe types but the elongated cylindrical rooted varieties. Sow these around the end of May, in the same way as the globe types, lift them carefully in November, twist off the tops by hand and then store them in boxes of sand in a frost-proof place.

Radishes

If ever any garden plant was designed for simplicity of growing, it is the radish, which is the reason why it is almost invariably included among children's seed collections. Radishes grow very rapidly and are ready in about four or five weeks from sowing another advantage from the child's point of view, as children love instant plants – but they must be supplied with plenty of water if they are to remain crisp and tasty. Once the radishes are the size of a quarter, begin to harvest quickly because if they stay in the ground too long they will become woody and bitter, particularly if the weather starts to get very warm.

Sow the seeds thinly in rows about 6in apart or in small groups in and among other plants in sunny positions. If thinning is needed, leave one plant about every inch. You can sow as early as late winter under cloches in pre-warmed soil but the best results will be from sowings made from early March onward. I am not convinced that it is worth sowing spring radish varieties after the end of May for they almost invariably run to seed. However, the spring radish varieties can be sown again in the fall once the days are shorter and the weather is cooler. The long rooted winter radish varieties are also well worth growing. Sow them from May until August, when they will mature in about ten or eleven weeks, and thin the rather larger plants to a spacing of about 6in.

The cucurbit family

It is easy to see why these vegetables, with similar succulent, somewhat watery vegetable fruits, belong to the same family, the cucurbits. In addition to sharing the same general form, they are all plants of essentially warm, moist but sunny climates. In recent years, zucchini has become the most popular of the group. It is easy to grow and, though it is a fairly large plant, it is also a very productive one. In fact, a well grown mound of zucchini will produce enough fruit for your household and some to share with the neighbors as well.

Zucchini are usually sown direct into the sunniest part of the garden after the danger of frost has passed. Like other plants discussed, the planting date can be moved up by a few weeks through the use of cloches. If you are using cloches, put them into position several days before actually planting the zucchini to warm the cool spring soil. When planting without cloches, a 1ft wide strip of black plastic placed over the zucchini row will warm the soil and control weeds throughout the season as well. A spade can be used to tuck the edges of the plastic into the soil to prevent it blowing in the wind. After the soil has had a sunny day or two to warm, the zucchini can be planted.

Zucchini seed is inexpensive so if you are eager to push the season, little is lost if the early sowings are killed by a late freeze.

To ensure good drainage, plant seeds $\frac{1}{2}$in deep on a mound about 18in across and 10in tall. Work the soil deeply under the area where the mound is built. This mounding is especially important on heavy clay soils and will help prevent root rot during the critical period when the seed is germinating. Plant five seeds several inches apart on the mound and, if they all germinate, thin to three. Zucchini need plenty of room; a single mound will eventually grow to be 5 or 6 feet across.

Both male and female flowers are necessary for zucchini (and other cucurbits as well) so the first flowers are not likely to set fruit. In time each plant will produce both male and female flowers. So do not worry if the first few flowers fail, plenty of fertile female flowers and their male pollinators will soon follow.

Pick the fruits when they are young. This is when they are most tender and tasty and picking will promote the production of new flowers and fruit. Watch the fruits closely as they begin to form because they will grow amazingly fast in the summer sun. If you wait too long you will have a zucchini that is more suited for use as a baseball bat than a casserole.

Zucchini are subject to borers which may cause the plants to collapse in the mid-summer. Therefore, later sowings are usually necessary for a reliable crop in the late summer or early fall. It is easier and safer to use successive plantings than to resort to toxic sprays. In the fall be sure to clear up and remove all cucurbit foliage and stems to help control next year's borers.

Golden summer squash is grown just like zucchini. If space is limited you might not need both. But golden squash is fun to grow for picking when it is very young to color up a green salad.

Cucumbers

An amazing variety of cucumbers are available from most seed companies. There are the traditional vines, bush forms, pickling varieties, and even burpless hybrids for those with weak stomachs. Their culture is easy and no different from zucchini. Vining forms are usually grown on a trellis or netting though, to obtain the best quality fruit and to save space. They will become quite heavy by mid-summer so use a sturdy support system. Like zucchini, cucumbers are best harvested while they are young and tender.

CUCUMBERS

If male flowers (those without the small swelling) occur, remove them or the fruits will taste bitter.

Tie stems carefully to support canes and pinch out the top when the plant has reached about 4ft.

Melons are grown in a similar way to cucumbers, but fruit must be supported.

Pumpkins and melons

Pumpkins and melons require plenty of space but if room is available they can be very rewarding. Since their fruits are so large, they are not easily grown on trellises, so they need plenty of ground over which to spread. Nothing can match the sweet, rich flavor of a vine ripened melon fresh from the garden.

Since the vines of both pumpkins and melon are such wanderers, it is best to confine them to a special section of the garden. The use of black plastic mulch or permeable landscape fabrics will ease weeding among the summer tangle of vines in the melon patch. These mulches will benefit the cucurbits by speeding the warming of the soil in the spring. Also, they help prevent rotting by keeping the fruits away from the soil. Rotting is not usually a problem, though, unless the season is unusually wet.

Northern gardeners with a short growing season should select varieties that ripen early. Check with local experts for advice on the best varieties for your area.

Pumpkins and melons are a special treat for the children in the family. The vines grow quickly and the flowers are big and showy. They are great for demonstrating the role of pollinating insects in vegetable production. The flowers are soon followed by a rapidly enlarging fruit.

If you really want to dazzle the kids, select a pumpkin variety like Big Max that produces massive fruits. To get especially huge pumpkins, work well-rotted manure into the soil before planting and keep the soil evenly moist, but not overly wet, during the summer. Don't be surprised if you come up with a 100 pound prize-winning specimen. Imagine a jack-o-lantern that size sitting on your porch on halloween. But do not forget to grow a few of the smaller varieties, as it is these which make the best pies.

The plants of the cucurbit family are are moisture and warmth loving. Squashes (top left) and zucchini (top right) are always grown trailing because of their weight and this is even more true of pumpkins (above), which are much less likely to rot if the fruit are protected with a layer of plastic to keep them from direct contact with the soil. The toughest members of the family are probably ridge cucumbers (left), which can be trained either on the ground or on supports.

Bush and pole beans and peas

Neither bush nor pole beans are hardy, so they cannot be planted out until the frost danger has passed, although bush beans (top left and right) are sufficiently low growing to be protected by cloches at first. Pole beans (above and left) were grown at first as ornamentals, and even today the alternation of red- and white-flowered varieties will add interest.

Most gardeners will want to add at least some of the pea and bean family to their kitchen garden. All members of this family of plants have the special ability to convert nitrogen from the air into a form that they can use in the soil. Because of this, they need relatively little additional nitrogen fertilizer; peas, indeed, need none at all, but beans will benefit from a light application of a balanced fertilizer like 5-10-10 applied early in the season in accordance with soil test recommendations.

The dwarf or bush bean has the merit of producing a crop well in advance of the earliest pole beans, its only real disadvantage being that it is scarcely possible in a very small garden to grow sufficient plants – a total of about 33ft of row – to provide genuine continuity of supply. Bush beans are generally sown directly into their growing positions, principally because they are fairly large plants and grown in large quantities. These would take up a disproportionate amount of protected growing room in greenhouses or elsewhere at a critical time. They are tender plants, however, and if you want an early crop you must use cloches, sowing the seed about a month before the danger of the last frost has passed.

Before sowing, pack the seeds overnight in damp peat to encourage moisture uptake and aid rapid germination. It is sometimes suggested that the seeds should be soaked in water before sowing but this can encourage the transfer of disease from one to the others. The seeds are large and should be sown in twos, about 2in deep, each pair about 8in apart and in rows 16in apart. Remove the weaker of the two seedlings if both emerge. The cloches should remain in place until the beans threaten to raise the roof.

Pole beans

Pole beans are so easy to grow, giving such a high yield in such a small area for such a long time, and it is hard to find really fresh beans in the store. You will need fewer pole bean than bush bean plants so there is usually room to germinate some of the seeds and raise the young plants under cover. They are usually sown outdoors but because they grow so rapidly it is scarcely practicable to sow them under cloches, and outdoor sowings are usually delayed until about ten days or two weeks before the danger of the last frost has passed.

The key to successful pole bean growing is to provide the plants with a cool, moist root run. This is best achieved by preparing a 16in deep trench well in advance (the previous fall if possible) and thoroughly incorporating generous amounts of well-rotted manure or compost. The precise shape of the trench depends on the manner in which the plants are to be supported – on rows of canes, strings or around a wigwam structure. Whichever method you choose, place two plants or seeds either side of each upright support, water generously and then pinch out the tops when they reach the tops of the supports in order to encourage flower and pod formation.

Peas

Peas are more fickle than beans and give a fairly small yield in relation to their growing area, but fresh peas taste so delicious that I have made some room for them on the cropping plan. Concentrate on a few rows of hardy first early peas, sowing them in February under cloches. Remove the cloches and provide twigs or netting supports when the young plants are 2in tall.

It is important to plant peas early because they grow best in cold weather and are damaged by the heat in late spring and early summer. In recent years many gardeners have switched to sugar snap peas. These peas with edible pods produce a more reliable crop than the traditional pea.

SUPPORTING POLE BEANS

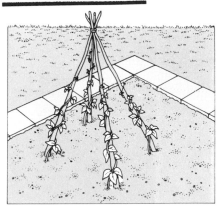

For a restricted area, a wigwam of three or four canes with two plants at the base of each is simplest.

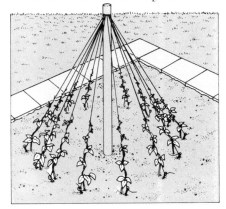

For more plants, place one at the base of the strings of a maypole, each string secured with skewers.

Crossed canes, braced against a horizontal, give a support frame that can be repeated several times.

Space-taking vegetables

Early potatoes, corn and broccoli and cauliflower – all take up a considerable amount of space and, with potatoes, this is a very sound reason for not bothering at all with the main crop, concentrating instead on the more exciting early potatoes.

Choose a plot that is sunny and has been well manured or composted in the previous fall. Add a general purpose fertilizer and plant between early March and mid April, depending on the relative mildness of your area. The planting material for potatoes is a tuber, often called a 'seed potato'. Intrinsically, this is no different from the tubers that you buy to peel, cook and eat but with the difference that the crop from which it has been obtained was grown to ensure a fairly uniform crop of fairly small tubers. Such high quality tubers are called certified seed potatoes and, in general, it is these that should be planted in gardens, rather than leftover potatoes from the grocery store. Sometimes grocery store potatoes are treated to retard sprouting.

Buy your seed potatoes as early in the New Year as possible and lay them on flats with the 'eyes' or buds uppermost. Place the flats in a warm, well-lit room and the tubers will soon sprout. Handle them carefully in order not to damage the sprouts and plant the tubers in mid March, using a trowel, sprouts uppermost, in holes about 4in deep and 12in apart. Gently replace and firm the soil and then use a hoe to draw more soil in low ridges over the planting positions. As soon as shoots appear above ground, draw more soil over them as protection from frost damage and repeat this regularly until the plants reach the stage when the leaves from adjacent rows touch each other. Thereafter, water regularly and, in a mild area, you should have early potatoes about twelve weeks after planting. An alternative method, using plastic sheeting, is shown here.

PLANTING POTATOES

1 Plant the tubers about 4in deep in March or April, ensuring that the sprouts are uppermost.

2 If potatoes are grown under black plastic sheeting, slit the sheet as the shoots push upward.

3 To harvest the crop, simply lift the sheet. The potatoes will be on or close to the soil surface.

Corn

If you have only a small garden and relish corn on the cob by the score, remember this: each plant will yield one or two ears only. The plants should be grown in fairly large groups in order to ensure pollination of the flowers, and each plant occupies about half a square yard. Plant the seed directly in the garden after the danger of frost has passed. As the plants grow, 'hill' them by mounding 4in to 5in of soil around the base of the plant. This will help prevent the corn being blown over. Plant at two week intervals for a harvest succession.

Broccoli and cauliflower

As gardeners become more and more concerned with healthful eating, broccoli and cauliflower have been soaring in popularity. These cabbage relatives are cool season crops. Therefore, they should be started early indoors, hardened off, and planted out about four weeks before the frost free date. If you do not want to start your own seed, garden supply stores usually carry young transplants during the spring season.

A fall crop should be started about ten weeks before the average date of the first fall frost. Unfortunately, trans-

TESTING CORN

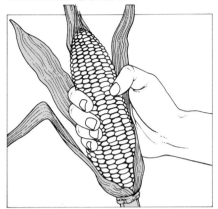

Test corn by pressing a seed with the thumb nail. When creamy liquid oozes out, they are ready.

plants are seldom available from garden supply stores at this time of the year, so you may be forced to start your own fall crop. Lightly sow the seed directly outdoors and then transplant the seedlings out 15in apart when they are big enough to handle. Both broccoli and cauliflower are fairly frost tolerant and can be harvested long into the fall until there is a hard freeze.

They are not heat tolerant, however, so be sure to harvest the spring crop as soon as the heads form. These vegetables are easy to freeze if there is too much to be eaten at one time, so store any surplus in this way.

TESTING BROCCOLI

Broccoli and calabrese are cut and come again crops – you can break off a small amount at a time.

Some vegetables are so bulky that in a small garden it is only possible to have token crops. Potatoes are worth growing for the flavor of the early varieties, and if space is limited they can be planted in a barrel or other container (far left). The annual calabrese (above), maturing in the fall, has replaced the biennial broccoli as a cut-and-come-again crop in many European gardens, but corn (left) gives perhaps the lowest yield in relation to its size: only one or two ears per plant.

Herbs

What cook worthy of the name can create savory masterpieces without fresh herbs? And I do mean fresh herbs; not the green sawdust that so often passes for the dried product on supermarket shelves. No garden is too small for at least the essential herbs, such as thyme, tarragon and parsley, and even my own herb bed, which is fairly comprehensive, occupies only about 11 square yards. Almost all types of kitchen herb are easy to grow, requiring little more than sunshine and fairly frequent watering but because they embrace a fairly wide range of plant types, they require a variety of different cultural techniques.

First, there are the herbs that are usually grown from seed: the annuals like basil, and the biennials like parsley and fennel. There is no real difficulty in growing any of these: the seed should be sown directly in the garden in spring, using cloches if the season or area is on the cold side. Basil is the only one among them that I would normally consider to be worth raising indoors until ready for transplanting.

Parsley is usually slow to germinate but there seems no logical reason why it should have earned a reputation for being difficult to grow. It certainly benefits from some lime in the soil, and pouring hot water over the seed sometimes persuades it to germinate more readily. Parsley is best grown on a short rotation – sow a small patch every year but allow the plants to remain for two seasons. They will produce flower heads in the second season and should then be dug up.

Fennel, once established, will self seed very easily and only the seedlings growing where they are wanted should be left. It has elegant but very tall feathery shoots and can be grown usefully in the mixed border if it is likely to dwarf the herb garden itself. You will see other types of herb offered

Herbs like thyme, parsley and chives can even be grown in containers if you don't have a garden (above), but they have special merits when grown outdoors close to the house (right), where they are usually raised in a more or less permanent bed in contrast with the more transient nature of other vegetables. In addition to their uses as food plants, herbs have the great virtue of being ornamental. Golden marjoram (left), chives, the many varieties of variegated thyme, purple leaved sage and the tall, feathery fennel are perhaps the classic examples of these dual purpose plants.

as seed but the flavor and general quality is almost always less than that of named varieties, bought as plants.

Mint is essential in any herb garden. The many different mints must be contained to restrict their spread but you should find space for a selection that includes not only the best culinary type, apple mint, but also black peppermint for your mid-summer drinks and eau de Cologne mint. This last is one of the most exquisitely scented of all garden plants – brush the foliage and then close your eyes for a real transport of delight.

Sage makes a small but attractive bush, the purple leaved form being perhaps the prettiest of the few available.

Thyme, on the other hand, presents an almost totally bewildering selection to the buyer. There are bushy and creeping forms, some vigorous and some less so, and several types with variegated foliage. Plant a selection for visual appeal by all means but sample sprigs carefully to choose the most aromatic for cooking; I find the silver variegated bush forms like Silver Posie the best in this respect, although they are less hardy than the all-green varieties and can suffer in hard winters. Indeed, it

makes sense to think of all thymes and sages as short term propositions and to take cuttings in the summer in order to have new plants to replace the old stock in the spring if the winter is severe.

Marjoram can be treated in a similar way; and it is well worth including the golden form in your collection to bring some really early spring cheer to your herb bed.

Tarragon, that essential accompaniment to chicken, should be reliable for several years in mild areas, provided it is given a little winter protection – peat mounded around the crown works well. If at all possible, buy the true French form, not the very much inferior Russian type.

Almost all herbs can be grown perfectly well in containers and a small collection of potted parsley, thyme, mint and chives, for instance, can be kept either in the greenhouse or on a kitchen window ledge to provide fresh leaves all year round. That biggest and grandest of the herb plants, bay, is probably always best grown in a large container rather than as a bush in the garden for it can then be moved readily to the greenhouse or a cool sunny indoor location in the winter.

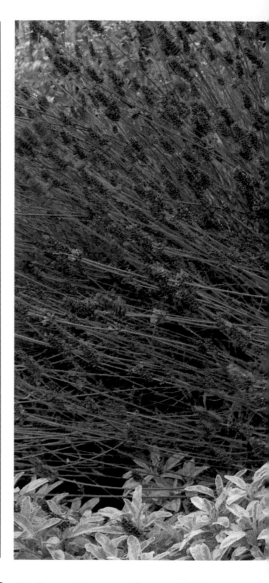

PARSLEY POT

A terracotta pot with holes in the sides is excellent for growing parsley, thyme or other herbs but people often have difficulties when they try to plant it through the sides. Instead, put potting mix inside up to the first hole and then push through the first plant *from within*. Add more potting mix to the next hole and continue to plant in this way until the entire pot is full. Then add three or four more plants on the top.

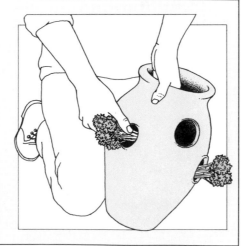

Herbs can be grown for eating, for ornament or for both – the lovely variegated sage, shown here with lavender and bergamot, is as edible as the plain variety. Other decorative herbs include rosemary, a useful evergreen (Rosmarinus officinalis forms a shrub about six feet high with either white, blue or pale mauve flowers), and the chive plant, which produces a cluster of attractive, clover-colored flowers.

MINT IN POTS

Mint can rapidly take over a herb garden. To contain it, use 10in or 12in diameter plastic pots filled with soil-based potting mix. Place one plant in each pot and then sink them to their rims in the soil of the bed. In the fall lift the pots and trim all protruding shoots and roots. Replace the pot for another year. Every two or three years, to keep a healthy stock of plants, pull off short pieces of runner from the parent plants and start afresh.

Apples and pears

Apples are one of the most popular of tree fruits, and are among the easiest to grow. It is surprising how soon in the life of a garden that a new tree, that has been nurtured and cosseted to its first joyous fruiting, becomes an accepted part of the garden furniture and in due course produces not only a sufficiency but actually an excess of fruit, to be forced upon friends and relations or, ultimately, to be consigned to the compost pile. Many gardeners acquire apple trees in full bearing and maturity along with the house and garden and so never pass through the stage of being able to choose and site their own varieties. The beginner to gardening can indeed find himself the owner of a plant that may be far older and possess far greater horticultural experience than he. If, on the other hand, you are not fortunate enough to have inherited an established tree, you will have the compensating pleasure of being free to choose your own.

There are several important matters to bear in mind. First, the apple varieties that you may have enjoyed from the store and always hankered to grow may not be suitable for your own garden. They may be foreign types, suited to other climates or even native varieties that only thrive in certain favored parts of the country. The flavor of the same apple variety can also vary quite markedly from one soil type or one climatic area to another, so before making a purchase, talk to apple growing neighbors and if possible sample some of their fruit. It is also a good idea to pay a visit to the nearest pick-your-own fruit farm where, although the varieties are likely to be restricted to those most viable commercially, you should at least gain an impression of how they perform in your area.

Having selected a variety, you should then make sure that it has a chance of bearing fruit by selecting another that is able to pollinate it. With very few exceptions, apples do not set fruit satisfactorily with their own pollen and must be cross-fertilized with pollen from another variety that flowers at the same time. Your nursery or garden supply store will advise you of a suitable partner for your chosen fruit and will also tell you if an existing variety (provided that you know its correct identity) growing in the neighborhood might be suitable. The only really reliable way of ensuring a good crop if you can only have one plant is to buy a family apple tree. This is a plant in which two, three or even four different varieties have been grafted onto the same stem. It gives an opportunity for those with gardens too small for more than one tree to have a range of dessert and cooking apples.

Dwarfing rootstocks

Whichever apple tree you buy, even if it isn't a family tree, it will be not one variety but two. The fruit that you have chosen is one of them, but the roots (or rootstock as they are known) is quite another. The reasons for this are two-fold; first because almost all apple varieties have been so carefully selected and bred for their fruiting characteristics that they have lost the ability to form a strong root system. And second, because through the careful breeding and selection of rootstock varieties, it has been found possible to govern the overall form and size of the tree as a whole. This is important, because by choosing an appropriate rootstock, you will be able to have a tree suitable for your garden conditions.

Most of the rootstocks that interest gardeners are called dwarfing or semi-dwarfing and result in small or fairly small trees (commercial fruit growers may choose vigorous or semi-vigorous types). When you visit your garden supply store or place your order with a nursery therefore, you should ask, not simply for 'Variety X', but for 'Variety X on Rootstock Y'.

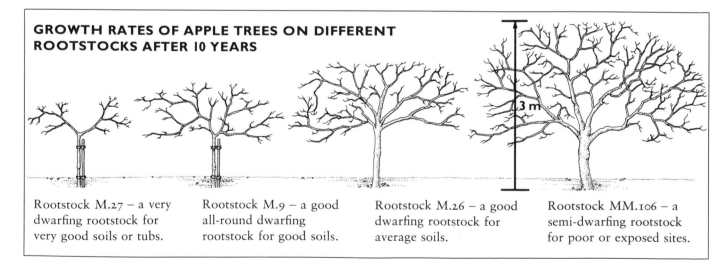

GROWTH RATES OF APPLE TREES ON DIFFERENT ROOTSTOCKS AFTER 10 YEARS

3 m

Rootstock M.27 – a very dwarfing rootstock for very good soils or tubs.

Rootstock M.9 – a good all-round dwarfing rootstock for good soils.

Rootstock M.26 – a good dwarfing rootstock for average soils.

Rootstock MM.106 – a semi-dwarfing rootstock for poor or exposed sites.

A tumbling old apple tree is a delightful feature that many gardeners have the good fortune to acquire with their gardens (left), but for those wanting to start afresh with new trees, there is now a huge choice of varieties. Many of these cater to marked regional preferences: Jonathan (top) is an excellent American dessert variety but less popular in Britain than Discovery (center) or the newer Greensleeves (bottom).

Also, dwarf varieties make excellent choices for growing in large tubs on a patio. These very small trees will need careful staking in the early part of their lives.

The best time of year to plant apple trees is in the fall or the early spring and if you order plants from a nursery these are almost certainly the times that they will be delivered. Container-grown plants from a garden supply store can of course be planted all year round but they will still establish best in the fall or early spring. Prepare the planting hole with care, as you would for any other tree: bear in mind that a healthy tree will be in place for many years, so it is worth giving it as good a start as you can. Never plant the tree any deeper than it was in the nursery. Dig a hole at least 50 per cent larger than the volume of the root ball, fork in well-rotted manure or another source of well-rotted organic matter. Take care not to 'glaze' the sides of the hole with your shovel since this will discourage the spread of the roots beyond the hole. Spread the roots carefully in the hole and insert a firm stake while someone holds the tree for you. The stake, of treated timber, should ideally be about 2in in diameter, about 8ft tall and with about 2ft in the ground. A belt-style tree tie should be placed about half-way up the stake with another about 6in from the top. (These should be checked annually in subsequent years and loosened if necessary.) Carefully return the soil to the planting hole with the compost, working it in carefully around the roots and firming it as you do so. Finally, create a broad 'saucer' around the planting hole to facilitate watering. Then mulch a wide ring around the tree with shredded bark or partially decomposed compost.

Once established, the tree should be

PRUNING AN OPEN-CENTERED DWARF BUSH

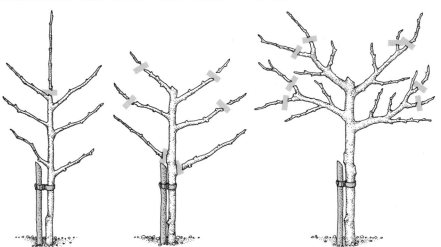

In the winter of the first year after planting a maiden tree (left), cut the main central shoot back to a bud or to above a lateral shoot at a height of 24in to 30in. In the second winter (middle) choose the four most evenly placed shoots and shorten them by about one-half, cutting each time above an outward facing bud. Remove other branches. In the third winter (right), cut back new growth on the branches by a half, again cutting to outward facing buds.

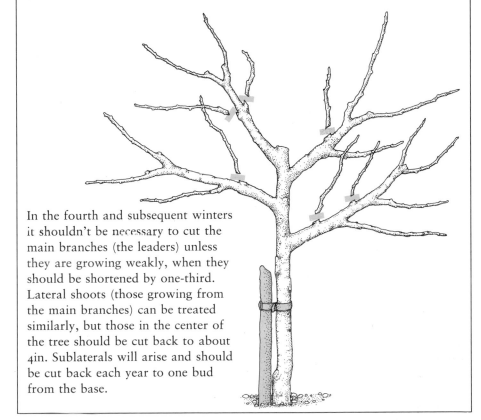

In the fourth and subsequent winters it shouldn't be necessary to cut the main branches (the leaders) unless they are growing weakly, when they should be shortened by one-third. Lateral shoots (those growing from the main branches) can be treated similarly, but those in the center of the tree should be cut back to about 4in. Sublaterals will arise and should be cut back each year to one bud from the base.

given a top dressing with a general purpose fertilizer in the spring, preferably using a mixture that contains a higher proportion of potash than nitrogen. Trees planted in lawns should not be grassed up to the base for at least four years. This reduces competition from grasses and prevents damage from lawnmowers.

All of this applies particularly to what are called free-standing trees; that is, those grown in the open, with no support other than a stake. But to obtain more variety within a small area and especially to provide the plants with some protection in an exposed

At one time, trees of the old dessert apple Lord Lambourne (left) would eventually have dominated a small garden, but by careful choice of a dwarfing rootstock, the same variety can now be grown in a tub or on a patio. Dwarfing rootstocks are also invaluable to the gardener who wishes to grow several fruit trees in a small space (above) by training them in cordons.

PRUNING CORDON APPLES

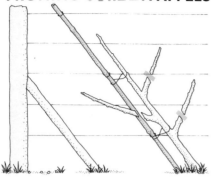

1 In the first winter, as soon as the young tree is planted, cut back side shoots over 4in long to three buds but leave the main shoot (the leader) unpruned.

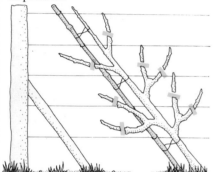

2 By the second winter, laterals will have formed on the side shoots. These should be cut back to two buds but the leader should still be left unpruned.

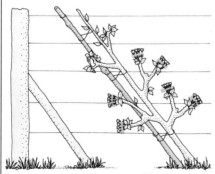

3 In the second spring, blossom spurs will form on the laterals. Cut off the flower buds as they appear but do not cut the growing shoots behind the flowers.

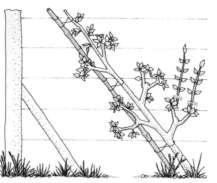

4 Late in the second summer, cut back lateral shoots longer than 8in to three leaves and cut back sublaterals to one leaf above their basal leaf clusters.

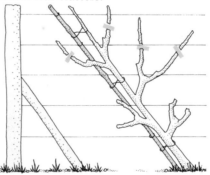

5 As an alternative to summer pruning, in mild, wet areas where growth continues late into the fall, cut back laterals to three buds in late winter or early spring.

6 Once the leader begins to exceed its allotted space, it should be cut back to about one inch at the same time as the summer or winter pruning of the laterals.

garden, apples can be grown against a wall, fence or training wires. Here, you should choose a fairly dwarfing rootstock, prepare the planting hole in the same manner but about 12in away from the support, and place the plant at an angle of 45° from the vertical. Apples grown this way are pruned differently from free-standing trees. For the latter, I believe that the simplest and most successful method in gardens is to train the tree to the form known as an open-centered bush, while the plants grown against a support are best pruned as cordons. The former is solely a winter activity but cordon training includes an important element of summer pruning too. There is absolutely nothing mystic or difficult about it and if you follow the diagrams, you should have no major problems.

As for the old trees that some of you will have acquired with your gardens, in many instances and if they are cropping satisfactorily, these can simply be left to fend for themselves, any dead, diseased or congested branches being cut away in the late winter.

On the other hand, if the old trees produce few fruit and especially if they are extensively cankered or otherwise diseased, their continued presence may well be to the detriment of any new trees planted elsewhere in the garden, which will themselves almost certainly become infected. In such circumstances, it would be very wise to remove the old stock if new trees are to be introduced.

Pears

And so to pears, first cousins of apples but generally much less popular in gardens. This is largely because of the feature summed up in the old adage about planting 'pears for your heirs'. Certainly they can take much longer than apples to come into full cropping but this traditional feature has been significantly diminished with the arrival of selected modern strains on mod-

THINNING SPURS

As the tree matures, the spur systems will become overcrowded. Thin them in winter to two or three fruit buds each and remove the weak or shaded flower buds especially.

The espalier (top) is arguably the most attractive way of training any fruit tree, and is a particularly effective treatment for pears. Conference (above) is popular in Britain and is one of the hardiest varieties of pear, while the variety Seckle (right), which is popular in America, produces delicious fruit, although it is not such a heavy cropper.

ern rootstocks. Most pears today are grafted onto quince rootstock. Many grafted pears bear at a young age; in fact, some varieties may bear a few fruits the first year after planting.

Pears respond particularly well to being trained as cordons where space is limited but, in general, their planting, care and pruning is the same as for apple trees.

You will hear and read a great deal about the pest and disease problems attendant upon apple and pear growing but, in reality, there is little that can be done about this. I feel that some pest damage to the fruit must be tolerated. Nonetheless, a fungicidal spray to minimize the damage from scab and mildew may well be worthwhile with young trees, on which the early season fungicides are much the most important. The timing of their application is critical: spray just as the young fruit is starting to form. On large, old plants, any sort of spraying is likely to prove a time-consuming and futile exercise, with the sole exception of a dormant oil spray applied while the tree is dormant and leafless in early spring. This environmentally safe spray will kill overwintering insects on and in the bark crevices. The selection of disease-resistant varieties will reduce the need for sprays.

Plums

Plums are another extremely popular garden fruit tree. In many ways they are even easier to grow than apples, as after the initial few years, pruning can comprise little more than directed neglect. Other features also make them particularly attractive, even for the small garden. Most of the best all-purpose plum varieties are self-fertile, meaning that only one tree is needed for a crop and although plums rather notoriously have 'off years' and 'on years', the yield in a good season can be prodigious. The introduction in recent seasons of new semi-dwarfing rootstock means that smaller trees can now be grown. Like most dwarf fruit trees, these bear at a young age.

The site requirements for plums are similar to those for apples and pears but they will never yield well in low areas as they come into blossom rather early, when their flowers can be damaged by a late frost. Planting is essentially the same as for apples but pruning is somewhat different. I recommend training the tree in the form of a pyramid as this generally gives the best results in gardens, but after the form of the plant is established, the amount of annual pruning can be diminished and mature plum trees can virtually take care of themselves at an earlier age than can apples.

There is just one very important point to remember when it comes to pruning plums: whatever pruning you do on your plum tree, it should be done in the spring and early summer; *never* in the fall and winter. The reason for this is a disease called silver leaf; a

In many ways, plums are much easier fruits to grow than apples for, once established (left), there is very little annual pruning. If you have room for only one tree, select a self-fertile variety like Victoria (top right). Damson plums (top left) are excellent in jellies and preserves and will also freeze well.

devastating and often fatal fungal infection. The spores of the fungus, by which it infects the tree through the cut surfaces of branches and trunks, are liable to be present in the air at any time from late July onward until the end of the winter. By avoiding these periods for pruning, you will diminish very significantly the likelihood of an attack.

One of the most troublesome features of plum trees is their habit of producing suckers from the roots. There is no ideal answer to this but it is always worse when the roots have suffered some disturbance such as that brought about by digging or repeated hoeing very close to the base of the trunk, or by the stress induced during a long period of dryness. If and when suckers do appear, they should be pulled away rather than cut, because cutting almost invariably compounds the problem and induces more suckers to form around the tree.

Some varieties of plum have a naturally spreading habit. In addition to this, plum tree wood is rather brittle, and as a result of these two factors the branches on old trees are very commonly pulled down and broken in the summer by the weight of the fruit on them. If you have acquired an old established and sprawling tree with your garden, don't be tempted to try to correct the habit by pruning. This will only result in a proliferation of leafy growth at the expense of fruit. Much the best solution is to provide props for the branches.

This is in fact a good practice in old orchards and avoids the mutilation of beautifully distorted old fruit trees that can add greatly to the charm of a garden. If the crop appears to be abnormally heavy, thin it out at the young fruitlet stage in late June (after the natural, early summer drop that is the method that all fruit trees use to dispense with at least some of their excess fruit).

PRUNING PLUMS

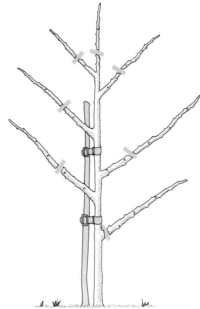

1 In the first spring after planting, cut back the main shoot (the main leader) to a height of about 4½ft, trim off any laterals below 18in and shorten other laterals by half.

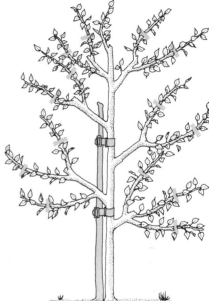

2 In early July, cut back the *new growth* on the branches to 8in, cutting to a downward facing bud. Leave the main leader and shorten laterals on branches to 6in.

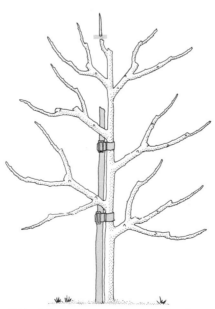

3 In subsequent springs, cut back two-thirds of the last season's growth on main leader. Once tree is 10ft, prune new growth to one inch.

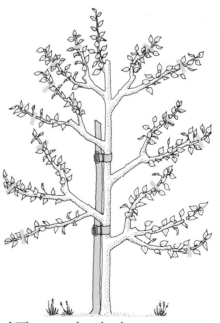

4 The second and subsequent summers, shorten all new branch growth to eight leaves and all laterals to six leaves.

Peaches and cherries

Peaches and cherries are closely related to plums, and all are members of the rose family. Since peaches bloom early, they should not be planted in low-lying frost pockets. Rather, they should be planted on hillsides with good air drainage. Also, like most fruit trees, they should not be planted in poorly drained wet soils.

Peaches are available in a wide assortment of varieties. Choose not only for taste but also for ripening time. Through careful selection, your peach harvest can last from early summer through early fall. All peaches are self-fertile so only one tree is required for a good fruit set.

Almost alone among fruit trees, good peach crops can be obtained on plants raised from seed — a harvest as satisfying to adults as it is to children. All you need do is to buy the fruit, plant the stone and raise your own tree.

Peaches can be planted close to a wall in the way described for cordon apples. Fit a pattern of horizontal training wires onto the wall, using eyes to raise them a few inches from the surface. If your soil is at all acidic, incorporate a light dressing of garden lime well in advance of planting and also give a top dressing of lime each fall thereafter. A soil test will provide the optional rates of application. The tree should be trained in the form of a fan. Like other fruit trees, the flowers will be pollinated by honey bees and other insects. Therefore avoid any toxic sprays when the flowers are being actively worked by insects.

As the young peaches reach about ½in in diameter, reduce them to leave one per cluster and then, when they are approximately golf-ball sized, thin them again to leave one for every 8in of shoot length.

Cherries

The major problem with cherry growing is that without some form of protection, you will share your crop

with the local bird population. Cherries can be grown in the lawn or against a wall. On the wall they can be fan-trained, in the same manner as peaches. Erect easily removable lightweight netting against the plants as the fruit begin to ripen. Most cherries need a pollinator but a few are self-fertile.

One of the most worthwhile sweet cherries to grow is the self-fertile variety Stella which can be obtained grafted onto a semi-dwarfing rootstock. At this size, the tree is small enough to grow in a cage where it can be left unpruned, apart from the removal of overcrowded branches.

Cherries are not the easiest of fruits to grow because birds enjoy them as much as we do. In recent years, their scope has been much extended because of the availability of the Canadian variety Stella (above left). Peaches, like cherries, are best grown fan-trained against a wall (top) where temporary netting is relatively easy to install as the fruit ripen (above).

FORMING A FAN-TRAINED PEACH

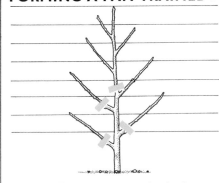

1 In the first winter, cut back the young tree to a lateral branch at a height of about 24in. Do not prune this lateral but shorten all lower laterals to one bud.

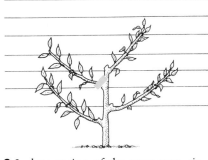

2 In late spring of the next year, tie in the topmost lateral pointing upward and the strongest on each side pointing outward at about 45 degrees. Cut off all other shoots.

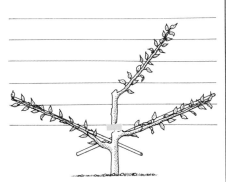

3 Tie in the two side shoots to canes and later in the summer, cut out the central shoot which has now fulfilled its purpose of building up a strong plant.

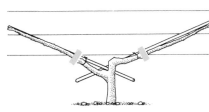

4 In the next winter, cut back the two side shoots to about 18in each, cutting to a strong bud. You may still seem to have a very small plant, but it will be a strong one.

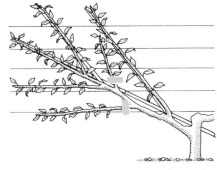

5 In the next summer, tie in four of the sublaterals arising from each side shoot (two above, one below and one extension) and cut back all other shoots to one leaf.

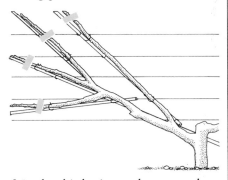

6 In the third winter, shorten each of the four trained shoots on each side of the plant by about one-third, ensuring that you cut to a *downward* facing bud.

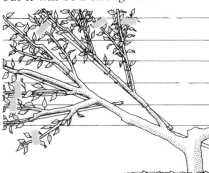

7 In the summer, tie in just three shoots from each of the eight laterals and in turn, later in the summer, pinch out further shoots arising from them at 18in.

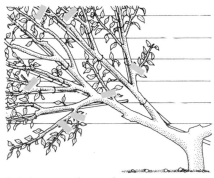

8 Subsequently, each spring, cut back to two leaves those shoots that have flower buds at the base. Also remove shoots growing toward or directly away from the wall.

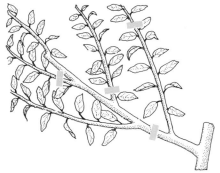

9 Choose two new side shoots on each fruiting shoot. Pinch them out when they reach 18in and, after picking, cut back the old fruited shoot to the best of the new ones.

Figs

Figs are among the most underrated garden fruit trees. They are very easy to grow in areas where temperatures do not drop below 10°F. In colder areas they can still be grown if given winter protection. Once established, they are almost indestructable. Pruning is straightforward, but the basis of success is laid at planting time.

Although figs can be grown as free-standing trees in warm areas, in most parts of the country, they are much better fan-trained against a warm south- or south-west-facing wall. Spring is the best time to plant a container- raised tree, because a young plant put out in the fall stands a high risk of being damaged by winter cold. The secret of good cropping later is in the site preparation, for although an established fig has an appetite for

water, it has little need for fertilizer and the knack is to confine its roots in such a way as to encourage it to produce fruit rather than masses of leafy growth. As a result, figs do not need the seemingly ubiquitous well-rotted manure or compost. Instead, the planting method is to excavate a hole against the wall of about one cubic yard and line the sides with concrete slabs. In the bottom of this pit, fork the soil surface and place a layer of rubble (lime-containing mortar rubble is ideal). Half-fill the hole with fairly poor, unfertilized soil and then plant the fig and complete the filling with more of the same soil. In future years, apply no fertilizer but give a thick organic mulch in the fall to protect the crown of the plant and conserve moisture the following year. Careful training of the

newly planted tree is important.

Select the three strongest upright shoots and cut them back to about 10in above the base late in the spring after planting. Two buds will develop on each to give six leaders which should be pinched when they have formed six leaves. This will stimulate more buds to develop and the shoots should be tied onto a pattern of horizontal training wires. In the second spring, the strongest of the leading shoots should be cut back to a point that will promote the development of the further side shoots that are needed to fill the allotted space on the wall.

Thereafter, the pruning is dictated by the fact that figs are produced on the young wood of the current year's growth. The aim of pruning is to encourage the development of new wood while retaining sufficient of the old to maintain a sound framework.

Start in the early spring by shortening any excessively long growths and cutting out any that are growing directly into or away from the wall or are crossing. During the summer, young figs will form and with luck these will ripen by the fall. Those that do not ripen will not survive the winter and can be pulled off or allowed to drop naturally. In the next spring, cut out the badly placed shoots as before and also a proportion of those that fruited in the previous year. Tie in new young shoots to replace them. It will take two years or so until you can judge accurately how much should be cut out each spring to maintain a balance between new and old wood.

After a hard winter, some shoots may well be killed by frost and the dead wood should of course be cut out and proportionately more young growths tied in to replace it. In northern areas, where temperatures drop below 0°F, fig connoisseurs wrap their trees in straw and plastic to give them extra winter protection. Brown Turkey is one variety that is hardier than most.

Figs are among the more neglected garden fruits, but with a little special care they can be grown successfully. In most parts of the country they must be placed where they have winter protection. Figs are therefore much more reliable when fan-trained against a warm wall. It is unwise to be too dogmatic about the pruning of figs, for in most seasons a proportion of the wood may be winter killed and it will be necessary to train in additional shoots to make up for these losses.

Grapes

Once established a grapevine will last for several decades, so it is important carefully to select the right grape for your needs. Specialty fruit nurseries offer a wide array of grape varieties for the home gardener. Modern grape varieties are complex hybrids with diverse parentage. It is not surprising that varieties vary in their adaptability to any one area; therefore, be sure that the selection you have in mind will grow well in your climate. Fruit catalogs usually give the critical information of winter hardiness and special growing conditions.

Each variety is usually bred for one particular use. For example, a table grape may not be very good for making jelly while a good jelly grape may not be the best selection for making wine. At the time of selection, know your priorities. By selecting several varieties with different ripening times, the season can be effectively extended. As with other fruits, great strides have been made recently in breeding disease resistant varieties.

Grapevines cannot stand on their own and need some support. They can be grown outside on arbors, trellises, or simply on three evenly spaced wires strung between poles 5ft tall. Use durable materials since the grapes will be growing on these supports for a long time.

For the first two years the vine will produce few grapes. During this time it should be carefully trained and pruned to develop a branch structure. Initially, a small stake is needed to get the vine up to the first cross wire. At that point, the vine should be pinched to encourage branching. The strongest branch should then be selected for training up to the second cross wire, where it is again pinched. The same process is followed up to the third or subsequent levels.

Once the structure is developed grapes will continue to need regular pruning. The most important pruning

TRAINING A GRAPEVINE IN A GREENHOUSE

To get early season grapes, a grapevine can be grown in a greenhouse, in the following way. In the first year, train the main shoot (rod) as shown – vertically and then horizontally, pinching it when it becomes straggly. Cut it back by half in the winter.

Next summer, thin lateral shoots on the rod to one every 18in and tie them up the roof slope. Pinch out sublaterals growing from them at one leaf. In winter, cut back all laterals to two buds and the previous summer's rod extension by half.

In subsequent springs, pinch out one of each pair of laterals, stop the other at the top of the trellis and stop sublaterals at one leaf. When the leader reaches its allotted space, treat it in the same way as a lateral. Leave one bunch every 12in and remove half of the bunches from each with blunt scissors.

Grapes can be ornamental as well as purely grown for food – train them in a conservatory or trail them over an archway for decorative effect.

is in the late winter or the early spring when the vines are pruned hard. Prune back to the second node on the wood produced the previous year. Also, remove any dead wood or crossing or rubbing branches. This will result in fewer but larger bunches of grapes and a vine that is more productive overall. As with other woody plants, make the cuts just beyond the node. Never leave stubs which can be an invasion point for insects or diseases. Later in the summer long overgrown branches can be cut back periodically. Grapevines produce best when planted in full sun and in good moist, but well drained soil. Most types can be propagated by layering: early in the year pin a portion of a lower stem (6in from the tip) under the soil with a V-shaped piece of wire. It should be well rooted by the next spring.

Raspberries

The number one soft fruit for most gardeners, raspberries offer an excellent, high yielding crop of very versatile fruit, to be used fresh, frozen or preserved. They occupy relatively little space, but like other soft fruit they should really be grown in a cage to protect them from birds.

Some people grow their raspberry canes with little, perfunctory, or even no support at all. This is a great shame, for the fruit yield is enhanced enormously by proper training, as much as anything because this protects them from the wind that so often causes fruit loss in free-standing canes as they are blown to and fro.

Buy raspberry canes from a reputable nursery or from a garden supply store that offers certified virus-free stock. Virus diseases are the bane of the soft fruit grower and even though he may not realize it, virus contamination is often the reason why plants gradually diminish in productivity after a few years. Certified virus-free stock will cost more, but the benefits far exceed the extra expenses. Choose a small range of varieties to offer early, mid-season and later fruiting (you will need about five of each to supply the average family).

Early spring is the best time to plant canes, ideally in a trench with compost or organic matter forked in to the bottom. Do not plant them too deeply; this suppresses the growth of new canes; plant them to the same depth that they were growing in the nursery. Spread the roots out and space the canes about 18in apart. Although the widely arching varieties require almost 6ft between the rows, it is possible to manage with an inter-row spacing of between 4ft and 5ft, the latter being preferable for the more upright or less vigorous varieties. Cut down any old canes after planting and give the plants a top dressing of a fertilizer containing potash – sulfate of potash, for example. Spread this at a rate of about 1oz per

Raspberries almost invariably require some form of netting as protection from birds, and a fruit cage (left) that fits unobtrusively into the remainder of the garden is the most straightforward way to achieve this. There are two main types of raspberry – the summer fruiting varieties such as Glen Clova (top) and the fall fruiting types, such as the American Fallgold (above), which offer a smaller crop later in the year. This variety has the additional attribute of golden instead of red fruit.

square yard in early spring, and follow it by a thick organic mulch.

After they have fruited, raspberry canes are of no further use, either to you or to the plants, and must be cut out. But it is no use expecting all of the new canes produced to bear fruit. Cut out with an old pair of pruning shears any that arise more than about 6in away from the row and also cut out the weakest to leave no more than six or seven strong ones on each plant. Keep down weeds between and within the rows for these will seriously deplete the yield; either use a contact weedkiller watered very carefully with a herbicide applicator or a scuffle hoe in dry weather. Hoeing must be done with care, however, for raspberry canes are essentially shallowly rooted and will be damaged by deep cultivation.

A dormant oil spray applied in the late winter or early spring is essential to keep the plants free from overwintering pests and their eggs. This will reduce the population of aphids early in the season but they are likely to increase later in the summer. Aphid control is important because aphids can inoculate your plants with viruses which they bring in from elsewhere. Insecticidal soap is a safe way to control aphids on food crops.

In addition to the normal early and later summer fruiting raspberries, you may also see so-called fall fruiting raspberries at your nursery. These produce two crops. The first matures in late June and is followed by a second crop which ripens in September, sometimes continuing until the first hard freeze.

The variety Heritage is one of the best 'everbearing' red raspberries. Where space is limited, it is a good bet because you get two raspberry crops in the space of one. Vigorous plants will often bear fruit the first fall after spring planting. To encourage a better second crop, keep the plants evenly watered throughout the summer.

SUPPORTING RASPBERRIES

Firm supports are essential. A series of training wires between stout, braced posts sunk at least 20in into the soil is the best system. Position the wires at 2ft, 3ft and 5ft above ground level and tighten the wires each season.

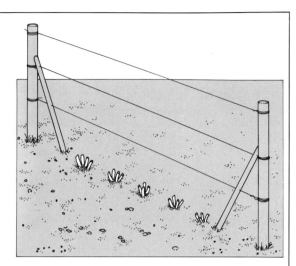

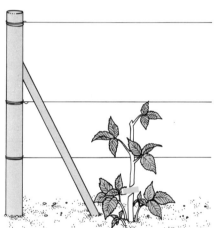

1 In the spring after planting, cut out the remains of the old canes which will still be present.

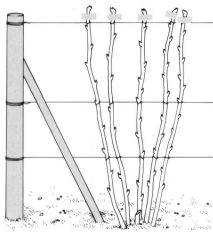

2 Long canes should be tipped back in spring to just above the top wire to stop the wind damaging them.

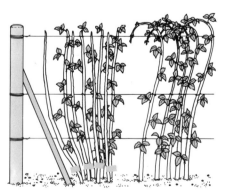
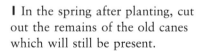

3 After picking, cut out the fruited canes, loop over the longest new ones, and tie them in.

4 In limited space, place one plant on each side of a single post and train six canes around it.

Blackberries and hybrid berries

Although closely related to raspberries, blackberries are trained in a slightly different way, partly because they are generally more vigorous and also because they produce pliable, not rigid, canes. Nonetheless, the general principle of cutting out the old canes after they have fruited is the same.

Although blackberries can be trained perfectly satisfactorily along wires stretched between two freestanding posts, I much prefer to position the posts and wires against one side of a fruit cage to give the canes extra support.

The planting, feeding and general care of blackberries are similar to the treatment of raspberries, but these are big, vigorous plants and need plenty of space. You can minimize the problems caused by this spreading tendency by choosing one of the more compact varieties and avoiding the real monsters like Himalayan Giant, but you will still need to allow a space of about 8ft between plants. Give them a dressing of sulfate of potash in the spring, then apply a thick mulch to help ensure that the plants do not dry out in summer. It is vital to water the fruit cage, for you will never have really juicy, tasty fruits without adequate moisture in the soil, as blackberries have a strong tendency to lose their flavor in dry conditions. If it is difficult to place the sprinkler in the fruit cage itself, you will find that it is equally effective to position it outside, next to one side of the cage.

The main consideration when training is to prevent the new and old canes from becoming enmeshed together in a hopeless, prickly tangle. There are several ways of achieving this but I have found the easiest system is the fan. After cutting out the old canes in the fall, tie the young ones onto the training wires in a fan pattern, but leave a V-shaped area of bare wires making about a 40° angle in the center of the fan. As the new young canes grow up in the following season, tie these into this

TRAINING BLACKBERRIES

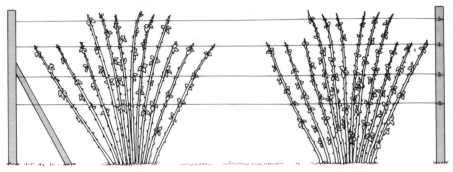

The fan system is the easiest one to use for the less strongly growing types and for those blackberry and hybrid berry varieties that produce firm, fairly rigid canes.

Re-tie last season's canes toward the outer part of the fan early in the year and tie in the new season's canes in the gap that they vacate in the center.

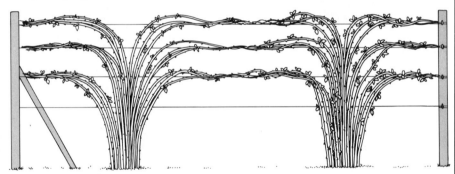

The alternate bay system is suitable for the slightly more vigorous varieties and especially for those that produce a large number of fairly thin, pliable canes.

Last season's fruiting canes are trained on one side of each plant and the new season's canes on the other, so that young and old alternate along the row.

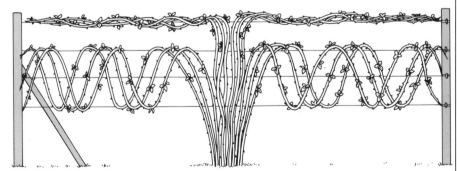

The weaving system is the one to adopt if you are growing very vigorous varieties and have plenty of space and also time to devote to tying in the canes.

The old, fruiting canes are woven between the lower wires while the new, young canes are arranged along the top and are re-tied downward in the following spring.

central area. When the old canes are cut out later, re-tie the new canes toward the periphery of the fan to repeat the cycle.

Hybrid berries

In addition to the traditional blackberry, there are many hybrids now available. Almost all of these are hybrids between raspberries and blackberries, but some have a related wild species as one parent instead. They have the growth habit of blackberries and should be treated in the same way but their flavor varies, and all differ somewhat from both blackberries and raspberries. There are many different types with rather splendid names like loganberries, boysenberries, tayberries and phenomenal berries. If you have a chance, sample the fruit before deciding which you prefer. It is also worth looking out for the many new varieties of these soft fruit that are becoming available to gardeners each year. Some of the newer varieties have the merit of an extended fruiting season, while others have the very desirable attribute of a lack of prickles – a very considerable advantage at picking time and when cutting out the old canes and tying in the new ones.

With new varieties like Darrow Cross (above), the blackberry has improved beyond measure in recent years to have large, firm fruit, more akin to some raspberries; but there are also hybrids between blackberries and raspberries that are certainly worth growing. The loganberry (left), seen here beautifully fan-trained, is one of the older types, and thornless varieties are available, while newer – and, in the opinion of many gardeners, better – is the tayberry (top), recently introduced from Britain and suitable for small gardens.

143

Fruit bushes

The average family will find that four black currant bushes are ample for their needs for both fresh and frozen fruit. Fall is much the best season in which to plant black currants, and the soil should be prepared beforehand in much the same way as for other soft fruits. A mature black currant bush is a big plant, and there should be a space of at least 4ft between each, although slightly less is permissible with the newer compact varieties bred specifically for garden use.

The planting technique is unique, for the intention is to stimulate the production of new growth from the very base of the plant and, to this end, bushes should be planted more deeply than is indicated by the soil mark on the stem. Immediately after planting, *all* shoots should be pruned back to the group of buds about 1in to 1¼in above soil level. This seems a heartless operation and means, in fact, that you will not have any fruit on the new bushes in their first summer, but it is a small sacrifice to make in order to give the plant a chance to build up a strong framework and crop well in future seasons. Feed and mulch the plants early in the year and continue to do so in all subsequent years.

Black currants bear their flowers and fruit principally on the wood produced in the previous season (which is why your new bushes will not crop in their first year), so the aim of pruning is to bring about the best conditions for a good crop by cutting out a proportion of the oldest shoots and branches, while encouraging new ones to form. After year one of growth, cut back any weak shoots to the base and also take out one of the stronger shoots in order to stimulate new growth. Thereafter, each winter, cut out any weak shoots and gradually take out a proportion of the old wood, cutting back each time to a strong lateral shoot arising low down or, if none is present, to the base. Among the old shoots, always cut out

Black currants (above) are large bushes, growing to an average height and spread of 5ft by 4ft. If you have a small garden, it would be better to choose one of the new, more compact varieties like Ben Sarek (right), which was bred in Scotland. In either case, plant deeply (below) to encourage strong growth.

first those that arise from the sides of the bush at a very low angle, for these will inevitably be dragged down to soil level with the weight of fruit on them.

Red and white currants and gooseberries

Because of the way that they bear fruit, black currants cannot be trained as cordons. Fortunately, this is an option with red and white currants or gooseberries, and cordons are often a useful way to economize on space in a small garden. These plants produce their flowers and fruit mainly on spurs borne on the older wood and also at the base of the shoots produced last

PRUNING BLACK CURRANTS

1 Immediately after planting, cut back all shoots on young plants to just above ground level.

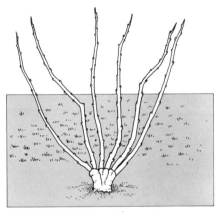

2 During the second year, strong new shoots will arise from the extreme base to fruit next summer.

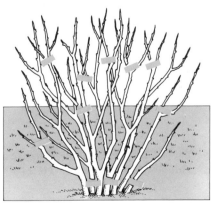

3 In subsequent seasons, cut back one-third of the shoots to the base after the fruits have been picked.

year, and they should be pruned in both winter and summer to promote fruitfulness. If you intend to grow your plants as bushes, place them about 4ft apart, slightly closer than you would with most black currant varieties. Again, four bushes will be enough for the average family. As with black currants, fall is the best season to plant, but do not plant deeply, only to the soil mark on the stem that indicates the depth at which the bushes were growing in the nursery.

After planting red or white currants, cut back each shoot to an outward facing bud positioned about four buds above its base. Cut off completely any shoots below about 4in to 6in from soil level. In the next two or three winters, shorten each of the branch leaders by about half, cutting always to an outward facing bud, and cut back the lateral shoots arising on these leaders to one bud from the base. In subsequent winters, simply continue to cut back the laterals in the same way and cut back the leaders to leave about 3in to 4in of the previous summer's growth.

Summer pruning is also important for otherwise the shoots can become overcrowded. It should not, however, be done before the end of June or you will be faced with a mass of proliferating side-shoots. For the summer pruning, pinch back to five leaves all of the soft lateral shoots of the current season (these are the laterals that you will be shortening to one bud in the winter), but do not touch the leaders at this stage.

I prefer to train gooseberry bushes on a slightly longer stem (or leg as it is called) as this makes picking easier. After planting, remove any shoots on the stem base up to about 6in above soil level. Many gooseberry varieties have a naturally spreading habit, rather than the upright form more characteristic of red and white currants. If your plants are of this type, prune the leaders by

half in the usual way, but take them back to an inward, not an outward, facing bud. Unless you do this, the weight of the fruit will later drag down and damage the branches. In subsequent winters, follow the guidelines already given for the currants, but again prune to inward facing buds.

Gooseberries, because of their very prickly nature, are not easy fruit to pick and it is important to keep the center of the bush fairly open. Thin out the shoots growing toward the center each year and from time to time prune some of the older branches rather harder. Summer pruning of laterals to five leaves after the end of June will also help.

Cordon training

Red and white currants and gooseberries can be trained as single, double or triple cordons. In each case, space the plants along training wires such as those used for raspberries, allowing about 1ft between plants for single, 2ft for double and 3ft for triple cordons. After planting, choose the one, two or three strongest shoots to form the leaders and cut them back by half to outward facing buds, cutting back laterals as shown.

To give adequate support to cordons, vertical canes should be pushed in close to the plants and tied securely to the horizontal training wires. The young leading shoots must then be tied carefully to these canes. In practice the pruning operation treats the cordon plant in the same way as a single branch on a bush. Soon after the end of June, pinch out all of the lateral shoots at five leaves. Later, in winter, cut these laterals back again to one bud, at the same time shortening the leader by between one-third and a half (less if it is growing very strongly, more if weakly). Tie the plant in regularly to the vertical support canes and then, once the leader has reached its allotted space, treat it in the same way as a lateral, shortening it to five leaves in the summer and back to one bud in the winter. On both cordon and bush plants, cut away in the winter any suckers that may have arisen.

Pest and disease control on black currants, red currants, white currants and gooseberries should simply be a matter of applying a dormant oil spray in the late winter or early spring. Any outbreaks that occur during the growing season can be treated promptly with insecticidal soap. Spray the affected leaves thoroughly as they tend to curl inward. Many currants and gooseberries are the alternate host of blister rust, a serious disease of white pines. For this reason they cannot legally be grown in some northeastern states. Therefore, check the local restrictions before planting.

Even if you buy the very best stock and take great care of them, virus contamination will almost certainly build up in the plants after seven or eight years and it makes sense to replace them, half at a time, after this period.

Blueberries

If you have a moist and very acidic soil in your garden (a pH of less than 5.5, as needed by rhododendrons, is ideal), you might like to try growing blueberries. These plants are unrelated to other soft fruit but have the same requirements for shelter from wind combined with plenty of sunshine. Plants are available at garden supply stores, but don't be put off by their rather high price: this simply reflects the fact that they·are slow to propagate. After planting, remove the young flower buds for the first season so that the plants build up a strong framework. Add a balanced fertilizer early in the spring, apply a thick peaty mulch and prune the plant lightly to shape. Thereafter, only a little light pruning will be needed. Blueberry shrubs are attractive, so plant them where they can readily be seen.

Gooseberries (left) and red currants (above) are both cultivated and pruned in a similar way. They are most easily trained as cordons, and the crop on the gooseberry shown here indicates that ample fruit can be produced in this way. For prickly varieties of gooseberry, this method has the advantage that the fruit are much easier to pick. The blueberry (top), Vaccinium corymbosum, *is only suitable for gardens with an acidic soil, but in addition to bearing delicious fruit it has the added advantage of being an attractive ornamental plant, with leaves that turn a brilliant red.*

PRUNING GOOSEBERRIES

1 On young bushes, shorten all of the branch leaders by half in the first winter after planting and remove any suckers that arise from the soil close to base of the plant.

2 On established bushes, cut back all of the current season's lateral shoots to five leaves in early July. Do not prune them before this or more side shoots will form.

3 In the winter, cut back to two buds the lateral shoots that you pruned to five leaves during the summer and also shorten all of the branch leaders by half.

PRUNING CORDON RED AND WHITE CURRANTS

1 After planting, shorten the main leader by half, cut back all of the laterals to one bud and remove any laterals that arise lower than 4in above the soil.

2 In early July (no sooner), pinch out the current season's lateral shoots at five leaves. Do not prune the leader but tie it carefully onto the support wires.

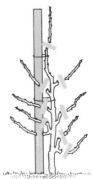

3 In winter, cut back the laterals to 1in and the leader to 6in of new growth. When it reaches the desired height, treat the leader in the same way as a lateral.

Strawberries

1 In late summer, pin down runners with young plants into small pots of potting mix sunk in the soil.

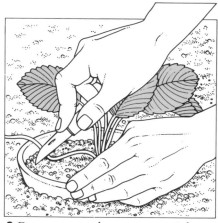

2 Do not sever the runner straight away but wait for about six weeks until it is well established.

3 After established plants have fruited, cut off the old foliage about 4in above the crown.

In recent years, several seemingly ingenious contrivances have appeared on the market under such names as strawberry barrels. They claim to provide a means of growing a good crop on a patio or similar small area, but unfortunately I do not know anyone who has been able to make them work satisfactorily, so I shall concentrate on the establishment of a conventional strawberry bed. If you do not have room for this, you can still enjoy your own, home-grown strawberries if you buy the continuous bearing small fruited alpine types, like the popular Baron Solemacher, and use them at the front of a mixed border.

The main requirements for the crop are a moist, water-retentive soil and plenty of sunshine. Cultivate the bed as thoroughly as possible in advance of planting and take care to remove all perennial weeds. Strawberries are not a long term crop and plants need replacement after two to three years, but they are poor competitors with other plants and can easily be overwhelmed by weeds even in that short time-span. Have your soil tested before planting and work in the recommended fertilizer when digging the bed.

You should always buy certified, virus-free plants but you have a choice in the time of planting – cold storage techniques mean that young rooted runners can be offered out of season. All the same I much prefer to plant in late summer with container-grown plants (buy the large or 'jumbo' sized plants if there is a choice). Planting at this time gives the new stock a period in which to establish itself before the winter and enables you to have a first crop in the following season. Spring

Strawberries can be produced, with varying success, in a container (top). plants in a conventional strawberry bed (left) should be considered as little more than short-lived perennials and renewed frequently. When the fruits begin to swell (above), lay straw beneath them to avoid the rotting that can arise from contact with the soil.

planting, however, can also be made very successfully.

Arrange the plants 18in apart in rows, allowing about 30in between the rows. Ensure that the roots are well spread out in the planting hole and then water them thoroughly. Everyone enjoys strawberries more if they are a week or two in advance of the neighbor's, so place cloches over the plants in early spring to give them this additional boost. I always give a very light top dressing of sulfate of potash at the same time and avoid using too much nitrogen as strawberries seem to respond by producing soft, disease-prone and fruitless growth.

As the young fruit begin to form, lay straw beneath the plants to keep them out of contact with the soil and minimize rotting and also to lessen the likelihood of slug damage. It is essential also to provide some form of protection against birds, and the easiest system is to use a purpose built, lightweight aluminum frame covered with nylon netting which can readily be lifted for picking.

After fruiting, cut off the old foliage with a knife at about 4in above the crown in order to encourage fresh growth to arise and build up the plants anew before the end of the summer. Runners bearing baby plants will soon appear but most should normally be removed as they will sap the vigor of the parent plants. A few plants can be kept especially for increasing the stock, however, and the runners can be pinned down for potting on. As soon as the crop in any season drops appreciably, it is an indication that virus has built up and you should then buy new certified plants.

Part 6

MAINTAINING THE GARDEN

In passing, while describing the various ways in which gardens can be designed, planned and planted, I have referred to fertilizers, weeds and weedkillers, watering and pest and disease control. In most instances, these references have been to specific problems but it is now time to think in more general terms about the way that your garden should be maintained.

One thing is certain: among the very first lessons that any gardening beginner learns is that his garden is far from static. No sooner do you turn over the spadeful of soil, put down the watering can or firm in the newly planted shrub than things begin to happen. The plants themselves grow and so deplete the soil of moisture and nutrient. At the same time they increase in size and thus begin to occupy an increasingly large proportion of the bed or border in which they have been planted. This, in turn, has a bearing on other plants growing nearby which will now experience increased competition.

As the plant grows, it becomes increasingly attractive to other organisms living nearby, some of which work in harmony with a gardener's objectives and some of which operate counter to these same aims. Gradually, and with experience, you come to appreciate these things and make allowances for them, but one fact is undeniable: the biggest feature contributing to the success of a garden is that your plants are grown with care and attention to their basic requirements.

Water is the key to keeping any garden attractive and productive.

Watering

Water is far and away the major component of protoplasm and this, in turn, is the major component of all plant tissue. Plants take up their nutrients from the soil in an aqueous solution and yet they also lose water constantly through their leaves; in the height of summer, one square yard of leaf cover may cause them to lose over 11 US pints of water per day. This must be replaced, and although it seems as if there is a limitless supply in the heavens, the amount of rainfall in summer is usually woefully inadequate. It must be supplemented in some way, and unless you are fortunate enough to have a well in your garden, this additional water must almost all come from your faucet.

Herein lies a doubt for the many people who realize that faucet water is chemically rather different from natural rain water. I don't believe that this should concern them; faucet water (fluoride and other additives included) is perfectly suitable for all garden plants, with the possible exception of really acid loving species like rhododendrons and azaleas; and even then only when they are grown indoors with no natural rain water at all. Limited supplies of rain water can, of course, be collected in a butt, although I prefer not to use this in the greenhouse because of the rather high possi-

COMPUTER WATERING

Watering controllers include devices that fit on a faucet and cut off after a measured volume, or this fully programmable timer.

WATERING SYSTEMS

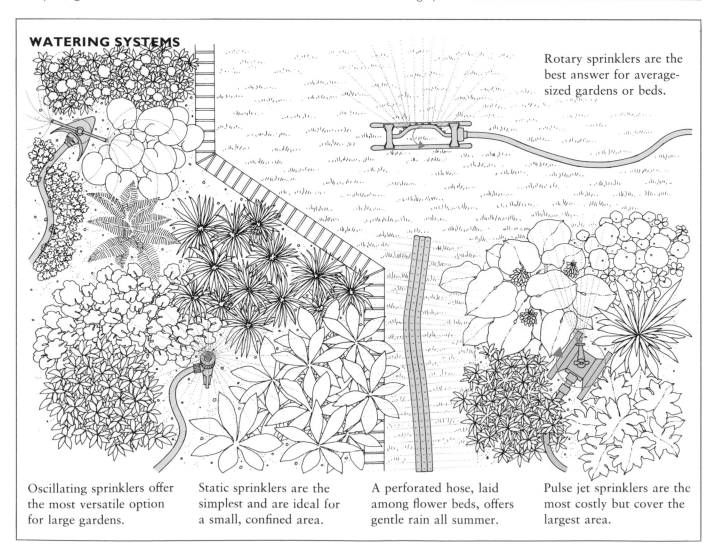

Rotary sprinklers are the best answer for average-sized gardens or beds.

Oscillating sprinklers offer the most versatile option for large gardens.

Static sprinklers are the simplest and are ideal for a small, confined area.

A perforated hose, laid among flower beds, offers gentle rain all summer.

Pulse jet sprinklers are the most costly but cover the largest area.

CAPILLARY MATTING

Lay capillary matting on a greenhouse bench and stand plant pots on this. A reservoir of water and a wick cut from a strip of the matting ensure that the potting mix never dries out, even when you are away from home.

bility that pests and diseases are successfully proliferating within it.

For your faucet water, you will, of course, need some form of delivery system and, unless you have a very small garden, a watering can will soon reveal its limitations. Garden sprinkler systems are now offered in a fairly bewildering variety of designs but before selecting one, check the pattern of spread that it offers and also the time taken to deliver a given quantity of water. Beware of being over-ambitious: a sprinkler covering too large an area can be very annoying to your neighbors.

Watering can become a particularly tiresome chore in the greenhouse. Although the watering can is satisfactory from day to day, problems arise when you are away on vacation. A helpful neighbor is an excellent investment but less imposition is offered by capillary matting. This is a form of water absorbent carpet that is designed to be laid over the pot bench and connected by a simple wick to a water reservoir. Rather more sophisticated is a trickle irrigation system which comprises a series of very narrow bore pipes, one being placed in each pot (this requires, of course, a water line nearby).

If you are away, the system can be connected to one of the devices for regulating water flow that are sold for garden use. These range from a simple faucet valve that can be pre-set to deliver a given volume of water and thus preclude the garden being drowned, to a sophisticated watering computer. Micro-processor controlled, this can be set in advance to deliver water for defined periods of time and at defined intervals.

The enhanced warmth and close environment of the greenhouse means that plants can soon dry out, so some form of watering system is a good investment.

Fertilizers and feeding

You will not garden for very long before you realize that while nature may manage her plants perfectly well without little bags of fertilizer, we expect rather more of our vegetation than the nutrients naturally present in the soil are alone able to provide. This is particularly true in the vegetable lot where we not only expect large and succulent plants, but we also expect the same area of soil to continue to supply the essential nutrients for year after year.

Plants actually take up nutrients through their roots in very simple chemical form and so the fertilizers that we provide must first be degraded

chemically in the soil to their more basic constituents. The three most important chemical elements needed by plants are nitrogen (indicated by its chemical symbol N), phosphorus (indicated by P) and potassium (indicated by K). These each have different roles to play and, although it is rather an oversimplification, it helps when choosing a fertilizer to remember that nitrogen encourages lush leafy growth, phosphorus is excellent in promoting root development and potassium stimulates flower and fruit formation. When you look at packets or bottles of fertilizer, you will see the proportions of these three major elements indicat-

Both hydrangeas and astilbes have a high demand for water and the latter make good bog garden plants. Both plants will appreciate being planted in a moisture-retentive soil which has been enriched with an organic fertilizer. The blue garden varieties of the common hydrangea, Hydrangea macrophylla, *will not produce good blue flowers if the soil is alkaline, so to avoid this, add peat to the soil and apply sequestrene or aluminum sulfate annually. To preserve the color of pink varieties in an area with neutral soil, sprinkle ground limestone around the roots once a year.*

ed on the label and this provides a rough guide to their useful purpose – a bottle stating N 5%: P 5%: K 8% is likely to be best for flowering and fruiting plants, for example.

Apart from the three major elements, plants also need other important chemicals but in rather lower amounts. These are called minor or, in some instances, trace elements and they include calcium, magnesium, boron, copper and molybdenum. Far and away the most important of these trace elements is iron, as it has a special role to play in the manufacture of the green pigment chlorophyll. Because of this, I always include an iron-containing fertilizer among my list of essentials.

Solid or liquid fertilizer?

Having decided that you need fertilizers containing N, P, K and iron, there are two further points to be considered. Should you choose a solid or a liquid fertilizer and should it be an organic or an inorganic product? Whether you choose a solid or a liquid form is mainly a matter of convenience. Some find it easier to apply the granules while others prefer the liquid form. A wide variety of formulations are available in both liquid and granular forms. Each are available in organic or inorganic, immediate or slow-release formulations. Whatever form you choose, carefully read the label for precise application instructions. Liquid fertilizers are easily applied when watering and some people prefer fertilizing lightly each time they water. Also as plants are actually able to take up a small amount of nutrient through their leaves, foliar feeding with some form of hose-end fertilizer dilutor provides an effective means of achieving this.

The choice between an organic and an inorganic fertilizer is one that has received a great deal of prominence in recent years, although the arguments over their relative merits are a century or more old. Largely, I think, because

FEEDING

The most accurate way to apply solid fertilizer to a lawn is with a wheeled spreader.

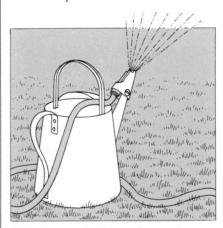

This hose-end dilutor fits on the spout of a watering can filled with concentrated liquid fertilizer.

An alternative hose-end system uses solid fertilizer pellets through which the water is drawn.

of the environmental contamination that has resulted from the excessive commercial use of chemical fertilizers containing nitrogen, the so-called chemicals have received a bad press. Although excessive use of any fertilizer is to be deprecated, I think that the relative effects of organic and artificial products on crop flavor are often overstated. Where many organic products score heavily is that they are slow-release in nature.

Basic fertilizers

Heading my list of basic fertilizers is a solid general purpose fertilizer containing balanced amounts of N, P and K (such as 10-10-10 or 20-20-20). This should be applied to perennials, shrubs and trees at the time of the first frost in the fall. Though the plants are dormant, their roots are still growing and absorbing minerals. A fall fertilization will result in a stronger plant in the spring. For annuals and vegetables, fertilizer should be applied at planting time in the spring: the best organic product is the mixture called blood, fish and bone. Second should be a liquid fertilizer containing a relatively high amount of potassium (such as 5-10-10) to use on rapidly growing flowers and fruits during the summer months. Third is bonemeal, an invaluable slow-release fertilizer rich in phosphorus and excellent when planting herbaceous perennials, bulbs, trees and shrubs. Fourth are two lawn fertilizers; one high in nitrogen to use during the fall to promote lush green growth and one lower in nitrogen, thus reducing the risk of diseases, to use in the spring and early summer. And finally, a fertilizer called sequestrene, which contains chelated iron, a form that plants can absorb readily from alkaline soils. Use this at the start of the season to prevent leaf yellowing, especially when soils tend to have a relatively high pH or on plants that grow best in acidic soils.

Pruning

If I had to name the most misunderstood of gardening skills – the one that is imbued with the greatest aura of mystery and mysticism – it would have to be pruning. This leads to a great deal of confusion, obscuring the fact that most pruning activities are governed by rules that are based on common-sense and simple logic.

Pruning is the removal of shoots, branches, buds, flowers or other parts of plants; usually, but not necessarily, from woody plants. One aim of pruning is to restrain the size of a plant: it may not matter in nature if a flowering shrub becomes 12 feet high and as many wide, but it is rarely convenient in a garden. Even though you may be aiming for a natural or wild garden, you are unlikely to want one species to choke or overshadow the rest.

As well as shaping and restricting a plant, pruning can be used to redirect its natural vigor into productive channels. Left to itself, for example, a tomato plant is an unkempt, straggly object, yet if you remove the side shoots you will induce it to direct all of its energies into one stem and form a plant that is not only kempt and digni-fied but also productive.

Take a look at any hedgerow or woodland and you will see plants rec-ognizably similar to those in your garden but many times larger and also growing together in a more or less tangled mass, in which plants are com-peting with each other for the available light, air, water and nutrients. More-over, the shoots and branches toward the center, starved of life's essentials, die and thus attract the attention of pest and disease organisms; so a third reason for pruning is to maintain the health and vigor of the plant through permitting a free flow of air.

But complementing all of these very sound reasons for pruning is one other, and this is in many ways the most important of all: when you remove some shoots, buds that are sited below

DEAD-HEADING

Rose When cutting off the dead flowering head, always cut just above the outward facing bud associated with the first leaf having five, not three, leaflets.

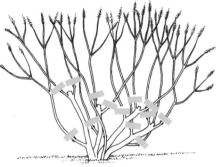

Buddleia Some late flowering shrubs, like *Buddleia davidii* (but not other buddleias), should be cut back hard to just above the base in February each year.

Wisteria Wisterias should be pruned twice; first in summer when the long whippy shoots should be cut back to six buds from the base and then in December to two buds.

TRAINING A STANDARD FUCHSIA

1 Select a plant with a strong straight stem and pinch out the top when the plant reaches a height of about 3 feet. Side shoots will then arise from the leaf axils.

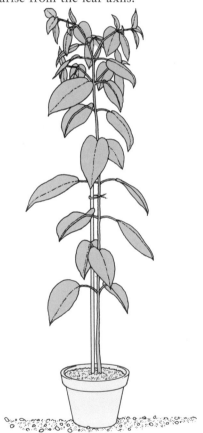

2 As the side shoots develop, pinch out those from all except the top three sets of leaves and then begin to stop these upper side shoots also to encourage a bushy head.

PRUNING CLEMATIS

There are three main systems:

1 The early flowering species such as *C. alpina*, *C. macropetala* and *C. montana* should be pruned immediately after flowering to remove dead shoots and keep the plant within bounds.

2 The early, large flowered varieties like Nelly Moser, Niobe and The President, together with the Jackmanii group and the mid-season large flowered types, like Marie Boisselot and Duchess of Sutherland, should have weak shoots cut out in February and other shoots cut back to a strong pair of buds.

3 *C. viticella* and all the late flowering species like *C. tangutica* should also be pruned in Febuary, but harder, by cutting all the previous season's growth back to a strong pair of buds just above the base.

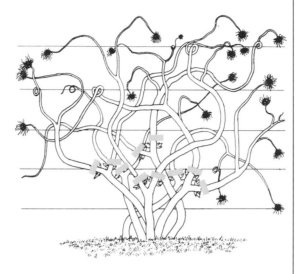

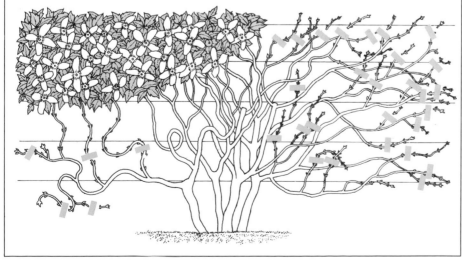

them on the plant, and that would otherwise remain dormant, are stimulated to burst forth. As a result, by pruning away the topmost shoots, we not only end up with a smaller shrub, but we have a more compact one as well. If the shrub is grown for its flowers, it will become a manageably neat and attractive flowering plant. If it is grown for its green shoots – a hedge for instance – there will be a neat, compact, many branched mass of greenery.

Incidentally, not all garden plants, nor even all garden shrubs, need pruning. Some are already so slow growing, small, neat, floriferous or otherwise amenable to cultivation that they manage perfectly well without.

The ideal time for pruning relates to the flowering time of the relevant plant. Flowering shrubs (including flowering climbers) flower in one of two ways. Either they bear their flowers on wood produced during the previous growing season or they bear them on wood of the current year. Those that produce their flowers on the old wood tend to do so early in the year, before the present season's shoots have fully developed. Conversely, those that bear flowers on the current season's wood tend to do so later, after mid-summer at least.

The early season, old wood flowers should be pruned immediately after the flowers fade. Only a few of this type require severe pruning and most need little more than a general tidying up of dead flower heads. Those that flower on the wood of the current season should be pruned at some time between late fall and early spring, the latter being preferable as newly cut shoots are not then being subjected to the rigors of a complete winter. Some of these do need rather harder and more regular treatment, although a good general rule is not to prune hard unless you are quite sure that it is desirable for this particular species.

Pruning shrubs

The following list summarizes the pruning system for the commoner ornamental shrubs, and relates flowering time to pruning time.

Berberis Thin out old wood in spring after flowering; shear hedges after flowering.

Buddleia Cut back *B. davidii* to four buds from the base in early spring. Shorten shoots of other buddleias after flowering to improve shape.

Buxus Bushes normally need no pruning. Shear box hedges in late summer.

Calluna (heathers) Shear old flowering shoots in early spring with hedge shears.

Camellia No regular treatment needed, but old, leggy plants can be cut back hard as the flowers fade.

Ceanothus (spring flowering) As a bush, thin only in spring. Against a wall, cut back to within two buds of previous season's growth after flowering.

Ceanothus (summer flowering) Cut back hard to within two to six buds (less for weaker shoots) in early spring.

Chaenomeles (Japanese quince) Cut out old wood, thin out and shorten side shoots after flowering.

Cotoneaster No regular treatment needed but rejuvenate old bushes by hard pruning in spring.

Cytisus (broom) Prune to shape each year after flowering, but do not cut beyond previous year's wood.

Elaeagnus No regular treatment needed but thin out and shape in spring.

Erica (heaths) Shape by removing dead flower heads with hedge shears.

Euonymus (spindle tree) Shape only during summer.

Forsythia Against walls, cut out old flowering shoots after blossom has faded. In the open, thin out only, every three years.

Fuchsia Large, hardy bushes are best given no regular treatment. Smaller and less hardy bushes should have dead growth removed in spring.

Hydrangea (mop-head) Cut out dead

flower heads in very mild areas but leave until spring elsewhere.

Hypericum Thin out in early spring. Vigorous types like *H. calycinum* should be sheared with hedge shears.

Jasminum Cut back flowering shoots of winter jasmine to within two buds of the base after flowering. Thin out summer jasmine after flowering.

Juniper Prune in late June and again lightly after the first frost if needed.

Kerria Cut out one-third of the old wood after flowering.

Laurus (laurel) Prune in spring; hard for old leggy bushes, less for vigorous young ones.

Lavandula (lavender) Cut back old flowering shoots in late summer.

Magnolia No regular treatment needed. Shape as necessary after flowering or in early fall.

Mahonia No regular treatment needed but remove long, non-flowering shoots and old wood in spring.

Philadelphia (mock orange hybrids) Remove old flowering shoots and thin out after flowering. Rejuvenate old plants by pruning hard in spring.

Potentilla No regular treatment needed, but cut out old wood in early fall after flowering.

Pyracantha (firethorn) No regular treatment needed for bushes in the open. Against walls, shorten secondary

shoots in summer and spring.

Rhododendron Very carefully remove dead heads after flowering. Rejuvenate old bushes by hard pruning in spring, before new growth begins.

Ribes (flowering currant) No regular treatment, but old bushes can be rejuvenated by hard pruning in spring.

Spiraea Cut out old flowering shoots after flowering (spring flowering types) or prune hard in early spring (late summer flowering types).

Syringa (lilac) Remove dead flower heads after flowering. Remove suckers annually. Rejuvenate old bushes by pruning back growth by up to one half in spring.

Tamarix Prune small bushes of late summer flowering forms hard in early spring. Large bushes should be shaped.

Taxus (Yew) Prune in late June and again lightly after the first frost (the same applies to hedges).

Thuja (Arbor vitae) Little pruning required. If used as a hedge, shear in late June.

Viburnum No regular treatment needed although *V. tinus* responds to shaping in spring.

Weigela No regular treatment, but remove leggy shoots after flowering.

Wisteria Shorten young shoots to six buds in July and to two buds in December.

A little pruning can go a long way for it will form and train plants into fantastic shapes that they can never have known in the wild. The standard fuchsia (left) represents just such an instance – so easy to form by careful removal of side shoots, yet so eye-catching to behold. But almost all flowering plants will benefit from some pruning, exemplified in its most simple state by the cutting back of old flowered shoots on winter jasmine (above) in order to stimulate further blooming the following year.

159

Lawn care

A lawn is a fairly easy area of the garden to maintain and is certainly the least labor intensive way of covering a given area with greenery, but it will not, of course, thrive with no attention at all, for like all other plants, grasses need feeding, watering and otherwise tending. In fact, as lawn grasses are the only plants in the garden that are grown with the specific intention that they will be walked on, it is not surprising to find that they have some rather special features among their requirements.

First comes the question of feeding, and I believe that lawns are best fed twice a year, in spring and in fall, using low and high nitrogen-containing fertilizers respectively. The mid-summer, so-called green-up fertilizers are very short-lived cosmetic treatments and I think that your money is better spent on other things, especially if the summers are very hot in your area.

You cannot really expect the best of the lawn if you miss either spring or fall treatment, but do be sure that you use each at the right time: a high nitrogen fertilizer used in spring can have seriously deleterious effects, producing soft, lush foliage at a time of year when this new growth is likely to be damaged by disease-causing fungi. The late fall fertilization is the most important one in most sections of the country. Though top growth is slowing down for the winter, the roots continue to grow and absorb minerals. The result is a thicker healthier lawn in the spring without an overly vigorous flush of top growth. Apply lawn food uniformly – a wheeled applicator for this purpose really is a sound investment if you have a medium to large garden. Do not use fertilizers containing chemical insecticides and weedkillers unless you know you have a specific problem that needs treatment.

Aeration is very important for a lawn that is on heavy, clay soil and for one that has withstood considerable

REMOVING IRREGULARITIES IN A LAWN

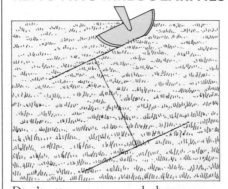

Don't attempt to remedy bumps or hollows by working from above. Cut H-shaped slots in the turf and peel the pieces back at either side.

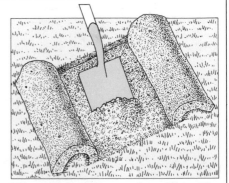

Then either remove soil or fill in. To aid re-establishment, mix a small handful of bonemeal with the filling in soil.

traffic during the summer months. Any form of punching holes in the lawn is better than none but a system that actually removes a soil core is much to be preferred.

In cool, moist areas, moss is every lawnkeeper's bane but efforts to control it should be kept within sensible bounds. No lawn is free from moss but I always consider a very mossy lawn as an indication of poor drainage, underfeeding, a very shady situation or, most commonly, mowing too closely. A shaved lawn permits light to reach soil level and thus encourages moss growth. It also weakens grass plants and ensures that they cannot compete with the moss and, in general, garden lawns tend to be cut much too closely. Lawnmowers permit adjustment of the height of cut and most domestic lawns should never be cut shorter than 2in. In parts of the country where bent grass is grown, this should be lower.

Lawn weed control is an emotive subject, for some gardeners believe that the presence of some weeds, particularly daisies, enhances the lawn's appearance. Certainly fine, weed-free turf is important for some formal garden situations. On the other hand, we are often too quick to use potentially dangerous herbicides on lawns as soon as a few innocuous wild flowers appear.

Keeping lawn weeds under control does not entail drenching the entire area with chemical. Individual weeds can be removed manually or really deep rooted perennials can be treated with a spot chemical applicator such as several manufacturers now offer. If you use the bagger on your mower, you will limit the dispersal of weed seeds.

In the garden on the far left, a strip has been left unmown, allowing attractive wild grasses and weeds to grow. The small lawn on the left has been made more interesting simply by curving the edges.

Weeds

Most gardeners will have heard the popular definition of a weed as a plant growing in the wrong place. There is nothing intrinsically bad about the plants we call weeds, but they happen, quite simply, not to be the plants we choose to grow. Because they out compete most of our garden flowers, fruit and vegetables, the weed species tend to flourish at the expense of the chosen vegetation. Left to their own devices, they will soon get the better of our garden plants, denying them light, nutrient and moisture, and ultimately overwhelming them through sheer vigor of growth or force of numbers.

In attempting to control weeds, it is important to understand why they are so successful. They succeed for one of two main reasons, either because they are very fast growing annuals that germinate, flower and in turn set seed again very quickly or because they are very deep rooted or far creeping perennials. The two types require rather different control methods.

Annual weeds

Annual weeds should if at all possible be controlled before they flower and set seed and the ideal way to achieve this is with a scuffle hoe which severs their roots just below the soil surface. But the hoe should only be used in dry weather when the weeds will shrivel and die quickly; in wet conditions, there is a good chance that they will merely be transplanted. In beds and

WEED AND PEST CONTROL

For careful application of weed-killer among growing plants, use a low-volume herbicide applicator.

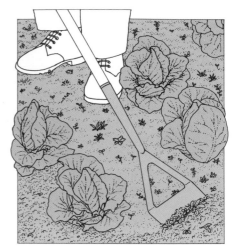

Never forget the value of a sharp scuffle hoe for weed control but use it only in dry weather.

The aerosol spray is too expensive for large areas but useful to pick out problem weeds in a lawn.

When applying any pesticide by sprayer, ensure that the undersides of leaves are covered with spray.

borders where the soil is subject to relatively little disturbance, a thick organic mulch will be an invaluable weed suppressor as well as retaining soil moisture. A mulch about 2in thick will suppress most annual weeds very effectively. Where weed seedlings do still emerge and when it is too wet to hoe, a contact weedkiller such as paraquat can be used. This is inactivated as soon as it reaches the foliage. Apply the chemical strictly according to the manufacturer's directions, preferably through a herbicide applicator bar which limits splash onto plants growing nearby.

Perennial weeds

For perennial weeds, contact weedkillers are of limited effect, for although they will kill the tops, new growth will emerge from below. The type of weedkiller needed is a translocated weedkiller — one that is absorbed by the plant and moved within its tissues to eradicate the roots at depth. The best known and most effective of these weedkillers is glyphosate (round-up) which will eliminate all perennial weeds, given time. Because of its need to move and accumulate within the plant, a period of a week or more may elapse before any effect is seen and even then two or three repeat applications should be made. But this is the only sure way to eradicate persistent perennial weed problems. Remember, nonetheless,

that glyphosate is a total weedkiller and will be taken up by all green vegetation, including valuable plants, with which it makes contact.

Lawn weeds

On lawns, a total weedkiller like glyphosate can only be used as a spot application or the grass will also be killed. The ideal lawn weedkiller is a selective one that does not affect grass but kills broad-leaved weeds such as plantain, dandelions and clovers. As with all weedkillers, the best results will be obtained if the chemical is applied during warm weather when the soil is moist. And on lawns, weedkillers are most conveniently applied with late summer fertilizer applications — several commercial brands of lawn fertilizer also include a weedkiller. There is a small number of lawn weeds, of which nutsedge is perhaps the commonest, that can only be controlled with difficulty by all modern weedkillers. To check the spread of these, several repeated applications may be necessary.

One group of weeds that can be a nuisance in lawns is the wild grasses that tend to appear, showing up as areas of a different color, and that can smother your chosen varieties. As these species are often too closely related to lawn grasses, you are unlikely to find a selective weedkiller. All you can do is to pull them out by hand or with a weeding tool.

There are a few garden weedkillers that should not be used among growing plants at all. These are the persistent, total weedkillers like sodium chlorate and aminotriazole that are blended for weed control on paths and driveways and which remain effective for a season or even longer. The existence of chemicals underlines the importance of reading very carefully the directions for the use of all garden weedkillers. It is all too easy to do heartbreaking damage by using a chemical for other than its intended purpose.

Always keep a watering can and sprayer, clearly marked, specifically for weedkillers. It may be tempting to use them for other purposes, particularly if storage space is limited, but equipment used for weedkillers should never be used for applying other chemicals on valuable plants. Traces of weedkiller can persist for long periods of time in the equipment and may cause severe damage if later used for purposes other than weed control.

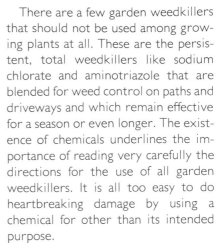

Almost every garden has a slightly different range of weed problems but you will be a very fortunate gardener indeed if you don't have at least a few of these common problems to contend with: lesser celandine (far left), dandelion (left center), sorrel (near left), bindweed (far right), couch grass (center right) or chickweed (below).

Pests, diseases and disorders

To define a pest is simple, to control it not always as easy. A pest is an animal that lives and feeds in our gardens in a way that is counter to our objectives – usually by eating a plant that we had intended for our own consumption or by so damaging a plant intended as an ornamental that it no longer fulfils its purpose. In common, I think, with most gardeners, I don't relish the idea of killing any garden creatures and limit pest controlling activities to those creatures that really have a serious impact.

Garden pests can be grouped into two main types in relation to the damage they cause; the chewers and the suckers. The chewers range from slugs, beetle larvae and caterpillars at the lower end to rabbits and deer at the upper. The suckers comprise a large group of closely related and very important insects including aphids, scale insects and whiteflies.

The chewing pests cause damage in an obvious and usually very conspicuous way, by eating visible pieces of leaf tissues, fruits, flowers or roots. The rather ragged holes that appear in broccoli and other vegetable leaves and betray the feeding activities of caterpillars are very typical of this type of injury. In many instances, it is the damage rather than the pests that is noticed and commonly the culprits have moved on by the time we realize what has happened.

The effects of sucking pests are not so immediately apparent, although in these cases it is often the insects that are noticed first. As their name suggests, they do not feed directly on plant tissue but withdraw sap from the plant by inserting a special feeding organ. In general, the damage is caused by sheer force of numbers: many hundreds of aphids, for instance, feeding on the sap of one stem will slowly and inexorably weaken it, bringing about distortion and general malfunction.

There are consequential effects from the activities of both chewing and sucking pests. The holing damage caused by the chewers can allow microscopic fungi to invade the tissues and bring about rotting or similar damage. The suckers, on the other hand, excrete a sticky liquid called honeydew that is not only unpleasant in its own right (as when it rains down onto people or onto cars parked under trees for example) but also attracts fungi called sooty molds which grow on the affected plants and quickly turn the honeydew into a black, revolting mess. Sucking pests are important in one more respect, however, for many of them carry plant viruses and spread these problems from an infected plant to others nearby. The gradual decline in potato stocks or raspberries, already mentioned, is a graphic instance of this.

Which pests must be controlled and which can be tolerated? There is a wide range of expert opinions, but I believe that most of the suckers must be considered serious enough to warrant direct action whereas most of the chewers cause little more than cosmetic harm. The chart on pages 168–9 lists the common garden pests and indicates avoidance or remedial measures, but some comments must be made about pesticides in general.

The choice of whether or not to use a chemical pesticide in your garden is yours and yours alone. I hope you will not be swayed too much either by manufacturers' advertisements or by nightmarish accounts of a world wholly devastated by pesticide usage. Used in moderation and with care, most of the pesticides sold to gardeners are not likely to lead to serious environmental contamination. All the same, some are more objectionable than others and I try to take a sensible middle course, as outlined below.

Chemical pesticides can be divided into those of contact action that kill pests when they make contact with them and systemic pesticides that are

Aphids (top) are the classic sucking pests, to be seen in large numbers on all types of garden plants in the summer, although the damage that they cause may not be apparent until later (above).

absorbed by plants and enter the sap, where sucking pests in particular are vulnerable to their effects. I never use systemic pesticides on edible crops because of the possibility that residues might taint the produce. And among contact insecticides, I try to avoid those based on organophosphorus or organochlorine, because these generally persist longer in the environment. Among contact insecticides, my choice lies generally with insecticidal soaps. In recent years, research programs have shown the value of these soaps. They are an easy and environmentally responsible way to control many insects.

Chewing pests take many different forms, ranging from the earwig (top) that hides in flowers during the daytime, to the larvae of sawflies which eat conspicuously on the surface of leaves (above).

One of the most common and serious fungus diseases is gray mold (top), which often infects through the flowers. Apple scab (above), by contrast, is difficult to control and must be tolerated in gardens.

Diseases

Microscopic fungi outweigh all other factors in the cause of plant diseases, and the numerous symptoms that gardeners soon learn to recognize are usually the manifestations of some parasitic fungal growth.

As with garden pests, so garden diseases shouldn't be used as an excuse to drench the environment with chemicals, and a measure of common-sense is needed before you instigate chemical warfare against the fungus world. With this proviso, there are some garden diseases that I consider to be important in the sense that some specific chemical control measure for them is needed. The chemicals available, grouped together as fungicides, are much more limited in type and scope than are insecticides and the former are generally less objectionable environmentally. Moreover, while there are systemic and non-systemic fungicides there is almost no likelihood of food crops being tainted by either form. Systemic fungicides indeed provide the only really effective means of tackling many plant diseases, for most microscopic fungi, unlike most pests, rapidly dive for cover and lie actually within the tissues of the affected plants where they are thus protected against direct acting chemicals. Even with a visible external mold growth, there will almost always be a corresponding mold development within the affected leaf or other organ.

In contrast to insect pests, the answer to much plant disease control lies in prevention rather than cure. Many of the most important garden disease fungi originate on plant debris left on the ground as a residue after pruning or other gardening tasks. This is especially true in the greenhouse where the generally favorable conditions for plant growth provide similarly favorable conditions for fungi to proliferate on crop remains. From here, they can spread to attack healthy plants, so my first tip for maintaining the health of your plants must be to keep your garden tidy.

The second tip is to grow your plants to the very best of your ablility, for a vigorous plant, like a vigorous person, is better able to shrug off the effects of any infections that do occur. And the third tip is to exercise vigilance, for during the height of summer, diseases can spread very rapidly and the sooner they can be dealt with, the better. Once disease symptoms do arise, they are often self-evident, for most people are familiar with the commonest effect, which is the appearance of mold growth. Small, restricted areas of moldy leaves or other tissues are best picked off by hand and disposed of or the odd moldy bulb among a batch thrown out.

One of the best means of disease control is the use of disease-resistant plants. Whenever possible, select varieties that have been bred and selected for their disease-free character. This is especially important for plants such as roses, apples, crabapples and tomatoes, which are normally relatively disease prone. Also choose plants well adapted to local growing conditions, as such plants are generally more

165

resistant to disease and insect attack.

Major outbreaks of disease can be handled as outlined above, but the garden diseases for which no treatment at all is needed far outweigh the others. Small blotches and spots, especially on leaves and stems, make up a huge bulk of minor diseases, all caused by fungi or bacteria but seldom having any serious effect on the plant. With the major exception of black spot on roses, I hope you will feel that almost all of these disfigurements are irrelevancies and cast no adverse reflections on your gardening ability.

I have left until last a group of diseases which is numerically small but which in many ways is the most important group of all. Virus diseases gradually bring about the decline in vigor of any plant species that is propagated by some means that entails the taking of some type of cutting, tuber, bulb, corm or other vegetative structure. Virus contamination is not controlled by chemicals, but if you keep aphids in check, you will help to increase the useful and productive life of dahlias, carnations, chrysanthemums and, of course, soft fruit bushes such as raspberries.

Disorders

A disorder is the name given to any problem affecting plants that is not caused by a pest or disease. In practice, many of the malfunctions that gardeners find on their plants every season fall into this category but are seldom recognized as such. Although a degree of experience is needed to differentiate some disorders from the symptoms of pest or disease attacks many others are straightforward to recognize once you know what to look for. The ability to distinguish the different problems is not simply a matter of academic interest, for the treatment for a disorder is quite different from that for a pest or disease attack. And of almost equal importance is knowing how to respond

Canker (top) is a serious disease of apple and other trees and like the less dramatic die-back (above) on roses and other woody plants should be pruned out, for it cannot be treated with chemical sprays.

to the various accidents that can befall plants, even in the best managed gardens.

It is easiest to think of plant disorders in two main groups; those that arise from some nutritional problem and those that do not. Nutritional disorders are essentially the signs that plants are being inadequately fertilized and although I have already outlined the importance of feeding them regularly, no-one ever manages to do everything correctly every season and it is useful to be able to recognize where things

Buds are delicate and prone to attack by diseases, like the bud blast on rhododendrons (top). Affected buds cannot be cured, although the very common mildew (above) can be checked by spraying.

have gone awry.

Nitrogen shortage is the most important sign to look for as nitrogen is the major plant nutrient. Plants especially prone to a shortage are the large, leafy vegetables like broccoli or spinach, the warning signs here being leaves which are reduced in size and pale colored, often with yellowish tints. In any vegetable garden where routine fertilizer applications have not been kept up, some plants will always be found showing these effects.

Plants can be damaged by non-living factors too – the weedkiller damage to tomatoes (top) and the frost injury on the young beech leaves (above) are typical of the type of damage that is commonly caused.

Phosphorus shortage is common on very acidic sites and also in areas with high rainfall, which tends to wash it from the soil. It also results in smaller leaves and generally weaker growth, but usually with some bronzing or a slight reddening of the foliage.

Potassium shortage arises on light sandy soils, and also commonly on alkaline sites. The effects are distinct and may take the form of a browning and shriveling of the leaf margins. Both phosphorus and potassium shortages can be avoided and corrected by rou-tine use of balanced fertilizers.

Shortages of most of the minor or trace nutrients are generally uncommon but there is one very notable exception: a shortage of iron is something that every gardener with a neutral or alkaline soil is likely to see in most years. The leaves of rhododendrons, azaleas, camellias and other acid loving plants, as well as raspberries and roses, show a marked yellowing but with the leaf veins remaining very characteristically dark green. Sequestrene contains iron in a form that plants can absorb even from alkaline soils.

Plant disorders may be due to a number of other factors, unconnected with nutrient deficiencies: among these, various climatic effects are especially important. Frost damage to young shoots in the spring appears as a brown scorching of the growing tips and leaf margins. Cold wind usually brings about an overall browning of plants, especially evergreens, and is often noticeably confined to the side facing the prevailing wind. Cold winter wind is the commonest cause of the browning of marginally hardy evergreens. In seaside gardens, this cold wind effect is enhanced by the presence of salt spray, which also causes the browning of foliage.

More severe effects brought about by the wind are the broken branches that litter gardens on two or three occasions every year after the passage of storms. Although broken branches cannot be replaced, it is important to give affected trees every possible assistance to heal the wound. Always cut back jagged stumps to a clean sawn surface close to the main trunk, but never cut a stub or tree branch flush with the trunk; cut to the small swollen collar that is present at every branch base. Leave the cut surface exposed, not painted with a wound sealing compound. It has been proved that painting the cut surface may actually hinder the natural healing processes.

Newly planted trees and shrubs should always be staked in such a way that they can sway lightly in the wind, but not so much that they rock the rootball loose. If a plant is staked too tightly it will never develop the strength it needs eventually to stand on its own.

Garden plants sometimes behave in very strange ways, and even if we can't always do very much about such happenings, it helps to know why they occur. As already mentioned, vegetable crops, like lettuce or spinach, have a tendency to bolt or run to seed and this invariably causes annoyance and frustration. Here the plant is simply naturally completing its life in response to the long dry days. Also, plants that have suffered a period without water and/or been exposed to a high temperature may bolt early. This represents a threat to their survival and they are therefore induced to produce seeds speedily, to perpetuate the species.

Blindness – the absence of flowers – occurs on a wide range of garden plants but is perhaps commonest on bulbous types, where it may be due to pest or disease damage to the bulb, to inadequate feeding of the plants after the previous flowering or to the bulbs having been left to dry in hot sun. Early removal of the foliage is the most common cause.

Sometimes, plants display bizarre shoot malformations. Often these result from a mutation in the growing tissues – the flattened and fused stem seen commonly on forsythias are of this type. But perhaps commonest of all is the thickening of the shoots and fern-like foliage that develops from time to time on tomato plants following the use of farmyard or stable manure. Such manures contain wheat straw and this usually contains traces of the selective weedkiller used by the farmer in the standing crop. Tomatoes are especially prone to damage from this type of chemical and respond accordingly.

PESTS	PLANTS AFFECTED	SYMPTOMS	CONTROL
Aphids	Most plants but especially serious on roses outdoors	Clusters of small, green, pink, gray, or black, winged or wingless insects secreting honeydew	Spray with insecticidal soap or contact insecticides as soon as colonies are detected. Repeat after three weeks
Mealybugs	Many indoor plants but almost always most serious on cacti and succulents of all kinds	Plants infested with fluffy, white insects	Touch colonies with paint brush dipped in rubbing alcohol. Spray with malathion
Scale insects	Many plants both indoors and out	Small colonies of stationary insects on stems and leaves. Some excrete sticky honeydew	Treat with systematic insecticide. Spray with malathion or insecticidal soap
Caterpillars	Many types of plants but especially on vegetables and shade trees	Rounded holes in leaves and fruit; small caterpillars may be evident	Pick insects by hand; spray with Orthene or use *Bacillus thuringiensis*
Spider mites	Many types of plant; especially serious on marigolds and other bedding plants in hot, dry weather	Plants become pale, bronzed or shriveled; sometimes with fine webbing seething with minute mites	Apply water mist spray to prevent mites from establishing. Apply insecticidal soap regularly
Whiteflies	Most indoor plants but especially serious on tomatoes, cucumbers, peppers and eggplants	Plants infested with masses of minute white moth-like insects	Spray with insecticidal soap or a commercial houseplant spray mixture; repeat every ten days
Black weevil	Rhododendrons, yews and other shrubs and ground covers	Leaves chewed along the edges, bark and roots chewed near soil line, legless white grubs present in roots	Spray and drench plants with Orthene or apply parasitic nematodes to control grubs
Thrips	Many flowering greenhouse plants, especially chrysanthemums, African violets, gloxinia and gerbera daisy	Flowers and buds with tiny fleck marks. Slender, tiny thrips may be seen deep inside blossoms	Ensure that plants do not dry out. Spray insects with malathion, diazihon, cygon or Dursban
Fungus gnats	Almost any type of plant likely to be affected when the potting mix is too acid or waterlogged	Tiny dark flies in and around compost; white, slender maggots with black heads around roots	Avoid over-watering. If damage appears, drench infested plants with malathion solution

PESTS	PLANTS AFFECTED	SYMPTOMS	CONTROL
Cyclamen mites	Many different types of plant, especially African violets, gloxianas, ivies, and foliage plants	Distorted flowers, leaves and shoots. Actual pests are too small to be seen	No chemicals are effective; potted plants can be emersed in 110°F (not more than 112°F) water for 15 minutes
Pillbugs, sowbugs and roly-polies	Many types of greenhouse plant but tomato and cucumber fruits are especially prone to attack	Stems of young seedlings bitten through; leaves and low-growing fruits may have irregular holes	Eliminate from under old boxes and beneath plant debris; use Sevin, diazinon or Dursban
Leaf miners	Almost all types of plant are likely to be affected. In the vegetable garden spinach and Swiss chard are often affected	Pale blotch-like or irregular meandering patterns develop within leaves	Pick off and destroy affected vegetable leaves; use Cygon or other insecticides on trees and ornamentals if symptoms detected early
Bulb flies	Narcissi, hyacinths and sometimes other types of bulbous plant	Distorted flower and shoot growth associated with presence of maggots or their damage in bulbs	Destroy affected bulbs promptly. After cutting off old foliage, rake soil over clumps to cover the holes. Use Dylex as a drench
Snails and slugs	Almost all types of soft, fleshy plant tissues	Irregular holes in leaves and other soft tissues; associated with presence of slime trails	Use brand-name slug baits or surround valuable plants with ashes or make barriers of spiny twigs
Wireworms	Almost all types of plants but usually most serious on potatoes and other root vegetables	Poor growth of plants, especially on old grassland areas. Yellowish slender larvae on roots	Cultivate land very thoroughly in winter to bring pests to the surface for birds to eat
Nematodes	Potatoes, bulbs, root vegetables and chrysanthemums are among many types of plant affected	Tiny yellowish bumps on potato roots, black rings in daffodil bulbs and knobbly outgrowths on root crops	Destroy affected plants and do not grow the same crop on the same area for at least four years
Sawfly caterpillars	Apples and other trees	Slug-like caterpillars eat leaf tops or caterpillar eats part or whole leaves	Spray or dust as needed with Sevin. Do not apply within one day of harvest
Cabbage maggot	Vegetables and bedding plants; especially at higher elevations and during cold, wet springs	Maggots on or close to roots and stem bases of plants with generally poor growth or wilting	Destroy affected plants and drench soil with diazinon around young plants when planting out

Part 7

THE GARDEN MONTH BY MONTH

I am often rather saddened when I visit people and their gardens in the winter. But not for the most obvious reasons: it is not the overcast sky, the rain, sleet or snow, the biting cold or any of the other features of winter's well-known charm that I find depressing. It is because all too often the garden itself has been forgotten; put away from thought, heart and deed with the last setting of the summer's sun. The end of barbecues for another year spells, it seems, the end of gardening interest until the spring. This is sad, because the winter garden air is especially bracing and there are still plenty of jobs to be done. It is also sad because a good winter garden has much to offer in visual appeal, much to tempt you outdoors to look, as well as to do.

Every season is different in the garden and one of gardening's greatest appeals is the changes in the forms, colors and perfumes that mark the passage of the year in a dynamic and continually interesting manner. In offering therefore this brief summary of the essential gardening tasks for each month, I hope you will not skip from October to April, from leaf sweeping to sowing seedlings, but will come to appreciate the seasonally cyclic nature of life in general, so that you will learn to use and enjoy your garden for all twelve months of the calendar.

Fall is the season when flowers give way to leaves and fruits with a whole range of colors that have no real counterparts earlier in the year.

JANUARY

Wash and disinfect all pots, seed flats, canes and other equipment put away in indecent haste in the rush of fall.

Complete winter digging in the vegetable garden when the soil is not frozen and is dry enough.

Check over and oil the lawnmower and other mechanical gardening equipment and, if necessary, have them serviced – later, you may have to wait.

Buy seed potato tubers as soon as possible and lay them out on flats in a warm, well-lit place for sprouting.

Cover a clump of rhubarb with compost and then place a bottomless pail or similar receptacle over the whole to force some early sticks.

Clear away leaves and other debris from alpine plants in trough and hollow wall beds.

Carefully shake snow from conifers and other evergreens to lessen the likelihood of branches breaking.

At the end of the month, sow seeds in warm propagators of plants such as pelargoniums and peppers that require a long growing season.

On a mild day, cut a few branches of forsythia for forcing; keep them in a cool room in water until ready for display.

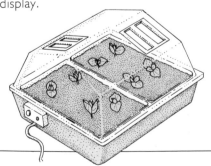

FEBRUARY

Check and secure stakes and fence posts loosened by winter storms.

Firm in plants loosened by the heaving of frozen soil.

In periods free from snow, take the opportunity to clear up fallen twigs and other debris on which disease organisms may thrive.

Ensure that an ice-free area is maintained on the garden pool but never smash the ice as the shock waves can harm the fish.

Check over stored dahlia tubers, bulbs, corms and any plants that are being overwintered and discard any found to be rotten.

Clear away wind-blown debris from snowdrops, winter aconite and other early bulbs.

Begin to lay in stocks of new fertilizers and composts.

Place cloches over strawberries to obtain the earliest crop.

Clear away the last remains of overwintered vegetable crops.

Toward the end of the month, place cloches over vegetable beds to warm the soil where the first sowings will be made in early March.

Apply dormant oil spray to fruit trees and bushes to kill overwintering pests, spraying when the temperature rises above 50°F.

Bulbs, with their in-built reserves of food already present below ground, are invaluable early in the year.

MARCH

Prune summer and fall flowering shrubs such as *Buddleia davidii*.

Begin outdoor sowing under cloches of radishes, lettuces, scallions, carrots, peas and other early crops and flowers.

Sow tomato seeds in propagators six to eight weeks before the frost-free date for your area for planting out later.

Sow annual bedding plants such as marigold, impatiens and others in propagators in warmth in the greenhouse or on a window sill.

Divide clumps of perennials that have become too large.

Fertilize spring bulbs as they finish flowering.

Prune roses, paying special attention to modern hybrid types (hybrid teas, grandifloras and floribundas).

Mulch borders while the soil is moist.

Fertilize and mulch soft fruit bushes.

Prune apple and pear trees as well as young plum and damson plum trees. Prune fall fruiting raspberries.

APRIL

Plant up hanging baskets in the greenhouse to have them ready for placing outside next month.

Hoe for weed control on dry days but use weedkillers when the soil is still moist.

Hill up early potatoes.

Lightly scatter slug deterrent around young shoots of delphiniums, lupins, phlox and other herbacious perennials. Take care to keep your pet away from slug poisons.

Prune and re-tie wall trained figs.

Sow or sod new lawns.

Plant summer flowering bulbs.

Cut back summer flowering heathers with shears.

Prick off all flower and vegetable seedlings as soon as they are large enough to handle.

Lift and divide waterlilies and also set up new pools.

About a week before the frost-free date, begin planting gladioli and sow green beans.

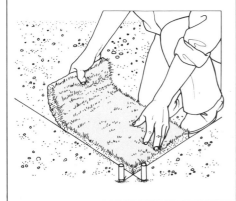

MAY

Plant out tomatoes, peppers and eggplants as soon as the danger of frost has passed. Be sure to stake the tomatoes at the same time.

Sow cucumbers, zucchini and other summer crops after the frost free date.

Cut back the yellowing foliage of the early spring flowering bulbs.

Continue to move bedding plants and vegetable transplants from the greenhouse to the frame for hardening off.

Stake and support herbaceous perennials before they become too tall.

Cut back early flowering rock garden plants such as aubrieta and prune early flowering shrubs such as winter jasmine and forsythia.

Begin spraying roses, as their leaves appear, with a combined insecticide and fungicide treatment for black spot, mildew and aphid control.

Apply shading compound to greenhouse glass.

Side-shoot and feed tomatoes.

Continue to hill early potatoes.

Plant out corn seed at the time of the frost-free date.

Take photos of your successes and problems to help with later planning.

Continue lightly to prune other shrubs as they finish their bloom.

Bright sunlight strengthens natural hues, making the early part of summer an exciting time.

JUNE

Use sprinklers or other watering aids to ensure that the soil in beds, borders and vegetable garden remains moist.

Place hanging baskets outside and fertilize regularly.

Lift and divide primroses and collect seed from them for sowing at once.

Lift tulip bulbs, if they need dividing, and dry them off in a shady, well-ventilated place.

Take semi-hardwood cuttings of shrubs like azaleas, forsythia and laburnum to increase your stock.

Ensure that strawberries and other soft fruit are well protected against birds.

Continue sowings of green beans, zucchini and other vegetables for continuity of cropping.

Tie tomatoes to their stakes.

Feed roses with balanced fertilizer after the first flush of flowers.

Lift and divide bearded irises as the clumps become overcrowded.

Dead-head rhododendrons and other early summer flowering plants.

JULY

Prune wisterias back to two or three nodes at regular intervals.

Take cuttings from pinks and carnations.

Apply liquid fertilizer regularly to annuals of all types.

Tie in new shoots on climbing roses and continue pest and disease control on roses of all types.

Stake gladioli before the flowering spikes become top-heavy.

Continue dead-heading of all flowers and pay special attention to sweet peas, which will cease blooming once allowed to set seed.

Remove pond weeds from garden pools by twisting it around a forked stick. Don't forget to feed the fish.

Cut off old foliage from strawberries after fruiting and pin down runners of any being kept to increase stock.

Complete any pruning of plum trees before the middle of the month.

Summer prune red and white currants and gooseberries and also cordon apples and pears.

Tie in new canes of raspberries, blackberries and other cane fruits.

Make sure the blade of your mower is set at 2in or higher for most grasses, to encourage deep rooting and help prevent scorching, especially in dry weather.

A mid-summer haze softens harsh colors.

AUGUST

Make notes or take reference pictures of any gaps or overcrowded areas in the mixed border — it is very hard to remember where these were later on.

Make final sowings of lettuces and other fast growing summer vegetables or cool season fall vegetables.

Prune flowered shoots from rambler roses.

Pot on any rooted cuttings so they have time to establish well.

Prune out old canes of raspberries as soon as all of the fruit has been picked.

Remember to apply a high nitrogen fertilizer to the compost pile to facilitate rapid decomposition of the large quantities of grass clippings, and add water if the weather is very dry.

Spray Michaelmas daisies with fungicide to prevent mildew.

Continue dead-heading of roses and other flowers.

Take softwood cuttings of roses.

Transplant rooted strawberry runners.

SEPTEMBER

Pick apples very carefully if they are intended for storage and do not keep any that are in any way at all damaged or diseased.

Sow winter lettuce in an unheated greenhouse.

Prune black currant bushes, summer fruiting raspberries, blackberries and hybrid berries.

If necessary, apply broad leaf weedkiller to the lawn.

Sow or sod new lawns.

Apply fall lawn fertilizer.

Plant spring flowering bulbs except tulips as soon as they become available.

Take bulb scales from lilies for potting up and multiplying your stock.

Take hardwood cuttings of shrubs for rooting outdoors.

Clean up the remains of outdoor tomato crops and other vegetables once they have been harvested.

A mixture of clematis varieties can give color from spring to fall.

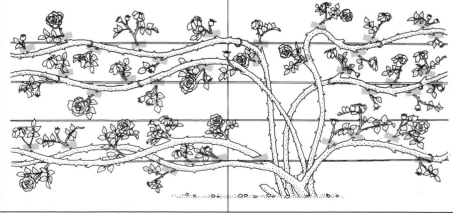

OCTOBER

Sweep or grind up leaves promptly and regularly before they block drains, cause paths to become slippery and deprive lawns of air and light.

Begin rough winter digging and fork in organic matter but leave large clods for the winter frosts to break down.

Construct or buy a compost bin to take the large quantities of old plant material available in the garden in fall.

Pot up a small quantity of mint to bring into the greenhouse or frame to give early shoots in the spring.

Lift dahlias, gladioli and other tender tubers, corms or bulbs to be stored over winter.

Complete trimming of hedges before the end of the month.

Lift and pot up geraniums, fuchsias and other tender plants to be kept in a frost free location over winter. Alternatively take cuttings before the parent plants are frosted.

Take soil samples of the vegetable garden and other important beds and treat as per recommendations.

Lift, move and divide large clumps of herbaceous perennials.

Fertilize trees and shrubs just after the first hard frost.

The unexpected fire of the witch hazel Hamamelis x intermedia *Ruby Glow, seen here flowering in February, benefits, like all winter blossom, from the clarity of the air and the stark contrast afforded by snow.*

NOVEMBER

Fertilize the lawn with a high nitrogen fertilizer. This is the most important application of the year, so if you only fertilize once, do it now.

Plant new bare-rooted, balled and burlapped trees and shrubs.

Check all stakes, fence posts and other supports before the worst of the winter storms arrive.

Plant tulip bulbs before the end of the month if possible.

Mound mulch, such as finely pulverized bark, around the crowns of roses and other plants that could suffer from penetrating winter freezes.

Fit bubble plastic or other insulating material in greenhouses and ensure that greenhouse heating equipment is working satisfactorily.

Complete lawn mowing and leaf grinding and clean and oil the mower before putting it away with any other tools that will not be needed during the winter.

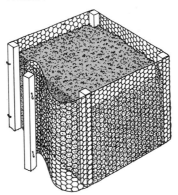

DECEMBER

Throw a small length of netting over berrying holly bushes to ensure that some are left by the birds and are available for Christmas decoration.

Check stored fruit and other produce and remove any that are damaged or rotting.

Place seed orders promptly with mail order suppliers.

Take root cuttings to multiply your stock.

Begin pruning apple and pear trees; spread the job over several weeks rather than trying to do it all in a hurry.

Sow seeds of alpine plants in seed flats. Leave these outdoors to overwinter, ready for the seeds to germinate when brought into warmth in the spring.

Lightly prune hollies and evergreens before the holiday and use the clippings for Christmas decorations.

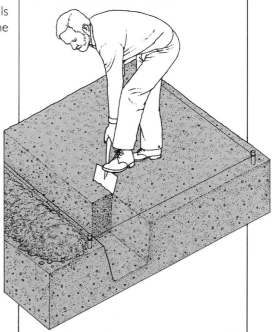

Recommended plants

These lists are by no means exhaustive, but they give a selection of varieties of the commoner plants that are generally found to be reliable and worth growing. Species of ornamental plants have only been included in cases where there are many named varieties, with significant differences between them.

BULBS AND SIMILAR PLANTS

Plant	Variety	Features
Spring flowering		
CROCUS (Dutch)	'Snowstorm'	Large, pure white
	'Pickwick'	Blue, with white stripes
	'Yellow Mammoth'	Golden yellow
DAFFODIL	'King Alfred'	Golden yellow, very strong and early
	'Mount Hood'	Pure white, long trumpet
	'Pheasant's Eye'	Small white flower with yellow-orange eye
	'Sugar Bush'	Miniature, white with yellow crown
SCILLA	'Spring Beauty'	Best color, strong deep blue
SNOWDROP		White flowers
TULIP	'White Emperor'	Strongest and best white
	'Black Parrot'	Extremely dark purple, frilled flowers
	'Greenland'	Subtly and strangely green and pink
	'Golden Apeldoorn'	Rich golden yellow
	All true species tulips	Generally smaller than hybrids, naturalize easily
Summer flowering		
DAHLIA	'Peter's Glory'	Pink, medium decorative
	'Yellow Show'	Yellow, large decorative
	'Cheerio'	Purple, white tips, small cactus
	'Lipoma'	Soft pink, pom-pom
	'Honey'	Outer petals rose, center lemon yellow, anemone
GLADIOLUS	Butterfly varieties	Compact, more resistant to wind damage than larger flowers
LILY	'Enchantment'	Rich nasturtium-red
	'Green Dragon'	White with green tinge, rich perfume
	henryi	Tall, large orange flowers, very easy
	regale	Pure white, very easy
Winter flowering		
IRIS *unguicularis*	'Marginata'	Violet blue, with narrow white edge

HERBACEOUS PERENNIALS

Plant	Variety	Features
Spring flowering		
BERGENIA	'Bressingham Salmon'	Deep pink flowers
PEONY	'Red Charm'	Medium red
	'Doris Cooper'	Pale pink
PRIMULA	'Wanda'	The best red-purple primrose
Summer flowering		
AQUILEGIA	McKana hybrids	Strong plants in wide range of colors
CARNATIONS/PINKS	'Doris'	Double, rose-pink flowers with darker center

Plant	Variety	Features
	'Blanche'	Double, white, fragrant
DELPHINIUM	Pacific hybrids	A range of strong growing tall plants in several colors, need staking
GERANIUM	'Claridge Druce'	Lilac flowers, very vigorous, good ground cover
	'Johnson's Blue'	Bright blue flowers like those of wild meadow cranesbill
	'Lancastriense'	Low growing over a long period with masses of pink flowers
GYSOPHILA	'Bristol Fairy'	The strongest growing double white
IRIS	Intermediate bearded and Border bearded	The most useful range for the mixed border
LUPIN	Russell hybrids	Strong plants in a wide range of mixed colors, need rich soil, do not do so well where summers are hot and dry
PHLOX	'Bright Eyes'	Pink with red eye
	'White Admiral'	The most reliable and strongest white

Autumn flowering		
HELENIUM	'Butterpat'	The best pure yellow
	'Riverton Beauty'	Yellow, with maroon eye
JAPANESE ANEMONE	'Alba'	Single white
HARDY ASTER		
(Michaelmas Daisy)	'September Charm'	Semi-double, deep pink
Aster x frikartii	'Wonder of Straffa'	Lavender blue, free from mildew and very reliable
SHASTA DAISY	'Aglaya'	Frilly double white

ANNUALS AND OTHER BEDDING PLANTS

Plant	Variety	Features
AGERATUM	'Blue Danube'	Compact, clear blue flowers
ALYSSUM	'New Carpet of Snow'	White, neatly low growing
IMPATIENS	'Blitz' hybrids	Tall, strong growing with very rich color
LOBELIA	'Crystal Palace Compacta'	Rich deep blue flowers on compact dark foliage
CALENDULA	'Bon Bon'	Compact pot marigolds in a range of colors
MIMULUS	'Calypso'	Very free flowering in color mixtures
NICOTIANA	'Domino'	Strong dwarf forms in a range of colors
PELARGONIUM (Garden geranium)	Ivy geraniums	Partly trailing forms for window boxes
	'Cherie'	Reliable, compact plants, salmon pink
	'Cherry Diamond'	Rich cherry red with well-marked foliage
	'Orbit'	Early blooming, flowered white
SWEET PEA	'Bijou'	Bush type, no staking needed
	'Old Spice' mixture	Mixed colors, very fragrant
	'Galaxy'	Mixed colors, summer flowering

ROSES

Plant	Variety	Features
HYBRID TEAS	'Alec's Red'	Cherry red, very full, very fragrant
	'Fragrant Cloud'	Rich orange red, full, very fragrant
	'Pascali'	White, small flowers, little perfume but very rain resistant
	'Peace'	Pale yellow, pink edged, huge flowers, little perfume but glorious
FLORIBUNDA	'Arthur Bell'	Yellow, strong, very fragrant, rain resistant
	'Iceberg'	White, vigorous, slightly fragrant
GRANDIFLORA	'Queen Elizabeth'	Rich pink, very vigorous, large flowers, slightly fragrant

RECOMMENDED PLANTS

Plant	Variety	Features
SHRUB ROSES		
Bourbon	'Mme Isaac Pereire'	Pink-purple, huge, shaggy flower, tall, vigorous, rich heady scent
Centifolia	'Fantin Latour'	Soft pink, double, shaggy flowers, very fragrant, exquisite
Hybrid Spinosissima	'Frühlingsgold'	Golden yellow, single, fragrant, vigorous, upright
Hybrid Rugosa	'Frau Dagmar Hastrup'	Shell pink, single, very fragrant, lower growing than most
Hybrid Rugosa	'Roseraie de l'Hay'	Rich deep wine red, double, fragrant, tall, a good hedging rose
CLIMBERS	'Aloha'	Rich coppery pink, repeat flowering, very fragrant, compact
	'Golden Showers'	Golden yellow, very long flowering season, fragrant
	'Handel'	Uniquely cream with pink edge, long flowering, slightly fragrant
NOISETTE	'Mme Alfred Carrière'	White, repeat flowering, very fragrant, vigorous
SHRUB	'Maigold'	Bronze yellow, rather untidy flowers but early, fragrant
MINIATURES	'Easter Morning'	Ivory, large flowers, good rain resistance
	'Magic Carousel'	White with broad pink edge, taller than most, very free flowering
	'Yellow Doll'	The best miniature yellow but care needed with black spot

SHRUBS

Plant	Variety	Features
LARGE		
BUDDLEIA	'Black Knight'	Long flower trusses of very deep violet
FORSYTHIA	'Spring Glory'	Pale sulphur-yellow blossoms, strong grower
HYDRANGEA	'Forever Pink'	Dwarf, with deep pink flowers
	'Blue Wave'	The best lace-cap and at its best when blue on acid soil
PIERIS	'Red Mill'	Good foliage colors and disease resistant, very hardy
RHODODENDRON	'Starry Night'	Purple-blue flowers
SYRINGA (Lilac)	'Ludwig Spaeth'	Deep wine red, single, prolific flower production
VIBURNUM	'Dawn'	Abundant, richly perfumed flowers, foliage reddish-purple in fall
MEDIUM		
BERBERIS	*thunbergii*	Scarlet fall foliage, red berries
CHAENOMELES	'Crimson and Gold'	Deep crimson flowers, golden centers, not too spreading
CORNUS alba	'Sibirica'	The best for red stem color in winter
EUONYMUS fortunei	'Sparkle 'N Gold'	Strong grower, attractive variegation
PHILADELPHUS	'Virginal'	Fragrant, semi-double flowers
POTENTILLA	'Katherine Dykes'	Strong, clear yellow blooms, compact plants
PYRACANTHA	'La Landes'	Hardy, orange-red berries
SALIX *discolor*	Pussy Willow	Furry buds in spring
SAMBUCUS *racemosa*	'Plumosa Aurea'	One of the best of all golden foliaged shrubs
SPIRAEA	*albiflora*	White, rounded flower clusters in summer
RHODODENDRON	'Boule de Neige'	White flowers
WIEGELA	'Bristol Ruby'	Strong growing, rich deep red flowers
SMALL AND DWARF		
CYTISUS	*decumbens*	Prostrate growth, yellow flowers
ERICA *carnea* (winter)	'Springwood Pink'	Spreads rapidly, clear, rose-pink flowers
	'Springwood White'	No other winter white comes near it for flower production
ERICA *tetralix* (summer)	'George Fraser'	Rose-pink flowers, grayish green foliage
LAVENDER	'Hidcote'	The richest purple flowers
RHODODENDRON	*impeditum*	Very compact, covered with masses of purple blue flowers
SKIMMIA	*japonica*	Very reliable berrying form with bright red fruits

CLIMBING PLANTS

Plant	Variety	Features
CLEMATIS	'Elizabeth'	Vigorous, pale pink flowers, perfumed, the best scented *montana*
	'Jackmanii Superba'	Vigorous, very free flowering, reliable, large deep purple flowers
	'Nelly Moser'	Old, reliable, lovely, very large mauve-pink flowers banded deep red
	'The President'	Seldom without bloom all summer, deep purple blue, silver reverse
HEDERA	'Gold Heart'	The toughest and most reliable variegated ivy, golden blotched leaves
	'Wilson'	Very hardy, resistant to leaf spot
LONICERA *periclymenum*	'Serotina Florida'	Rich perfume, compact growth through summer until frosts
WISTERIA *floribunda*	'Rosea'	Pink flowers, fragrant

TREES

Plant	Variety	Features
ACER *negundo*	'Flamingo'	Pink variegated foliage, the prettiest form of box maple
palmatum	'Dissectum'	The green cut leaved maple, fresher than the purple forms
platanoides	'Crimson King'	The best purple leaved tree
COTONEASTER	apiculatus – standard form	Arching boughs, green leaves, red berries, one of the daintiest weeping trees
GLEDITSIA *triacanthos*	'Sunburst'	The best small tree with golden yellow foliage
ILEX *altaclarensis*	'Golden King'	Easily the most reliable variegated holly
LABURNUM	*vossii*	Longest flower trusses of any laburnum
MAGNOLIA *soulangiana*	'Lennei'	Rich purple goblet-shaped flowers, the easiest magnolia
MALUS	'Red Jade'	Pink buds, white flowers, red fruit
	'Sissipuk'	Pink flowers, red fruit, resistant to scab and fire blight
PRUNUS *serrulata*	'Shogetsu'	Double pink flowering cherry
	'Shirotac'	White flowers, semi-double, fragrant
SORBUS *aucuparia*	'Scarlet King'	Scarlet fruit

FRUIT

Fruit	Variety	Features
APPLES, cooking	'Rhode Island Greening'	
	'Northern Spy'	Dual purpose, cooking or dessert
APPLES, dessert	'Golden Delicious'	Yellow fruit, crisp and sweet, good pollinator
	'Granny Smith'	Green fruit, crisp, juicy, keeps well
	'Mutsu'	Greenish yellow from Japan, a 'Golden Delicious' hybrid, excellent flavor
	'Macoun'	Dark red, aromatic flavor
	'Grime's Golden'	Golden yellow, spicy flavor, good pollinator
BLACKBERRIES	'Thornfree'	Fruits medium large
DAMSON PLUMS		Dark purple, good for preserves
GOOSEBERRIES	'Pixwell'	Hardy, few thorns, good for preserves
	'Poorman'	Large, red fruit, good for eating raw
PEARS	'Bartlett'	Good flavor but susceptible to blight
	'Moonglow'	Hardy, blight resistant
PLUMS	'Reine Claude'	Yellow fruit, excellent flavor

Fruit	Variety	Features
RASPBERRIES	'Newburgh'	Good flavor, virus-resistant
	'Heritage'	Ever-bearing, good for dessert or preserves
RED CURRANTS	'Red Lake'	High yield, good flavor, hardy
STRAWBERRIES	'Catskill'	Vigorous, large berries
	'Raritan'	Mid-season, good flavor
	'Ozark Beauty'	Ever-bearing, for cooler climates
WHITE CURRANTS	'White Grape'	High yield, mild flavor

VEGETABLES

Vegetable	Variety	Features
BEET	'Cylindra' ('Formonova')	
	'Burpee Golden'	Yellow color does not bleed in cooking
BROCCOLI	'Cleopatra'	Early autumn maturing, good flavor
	'Green Comet'	Late summer maturing, high yielding, dark green curds
BURPLESS CUCUMBER	'Green Knight'	Fruits 16"–18" long
	'Sweet Success'	Fruits up to 12" long
BUSH BEANS	'Tendercrop'	
	'Bush Blue Lake'	
	'Royalty'	Purple-podded
CARROT	'Chantenay Red Cored'	Quick growing for early and late sowing, cylindrical, blunt roots
	'Danvers Half Long'	Root thinner and longer than 'Chantenay.' Very sweet
	'Little Finger'	Early, extra sweet when young
CORN	'Early Golden Bantam'	Yellow kernels
	'Silver Queen'	White kernels, tender
GREEN ONIONS	'White Lisbon'	Reliable, good flavor, will last over winter
LETTUCE	'Valmaine'	Romaine, large upright heads, good flavor
	'Tom Thumb'	Butterhead, small, compact
	'Buttercrunch'	Butterhead, dark green, crisp yellow heart
MUSK MELON (cantaloupe)	'Burpee Hybrid'	Large fruit, orange flesh, good flavor
	'Early Crenshaw'	Salmon-pink flesh, dessert melon
PEA	'Little Marvel'	Early
	'Sugar Snap'	Edible pods, 'Sugar Bon' matures earlier and has bushier plants which do not need supports
	'Sugar Bon'	
PEPPERS	'Gypsy'	Early, outstanding flavor
POLE BEANS	'Blue Lake'	
	'Kentucky Wonder'	
	'Romano'	
POTATOES	'Superior'	Early
	'Kennebee'	Late
PUMPKIN	'Spirit'	Not as large as most, good flavor, pale green, striped
RADISH	'French Breakfast'	Round, fast-growing, mild, red and white
	'Cherry Belle'	Round, all-red, cherry size
SPINACH	'Melody'	Resistant to mildew, heavy yielder
SPINACH BEET or Swiss chard	'Lucullus'	Reliable, dual purpose (use leaf mid-rib and blade)
TOMATOES	'Gardener's Delight'	Small fruited, prolific, very sweet
	'Burpee's Jubilee'	Golden-orange fruited, sweet
	'Big Boy'	Large fruited, good for slicing, very popular
	'Big Girl'	More disease-resistant than 'Big Boy', good flavor
ZUCCHINI SQUASH	'Aristocrat'	Dark green, smooth, cylindrical
	'Gold Rush'	Yellow, high yielding, good flavor

Glossary

A

Acidic (soil) The opposite of alkaline soil, having a pH below 7, often a characteristic of peat.
Alkaline (soil) The opposite of acidic soil, having a pH above 7, usually a characteristic of soils containing limestone.
Alpine Plants predominantly from cool mountain regions, usually low growing and compact, typically used in containers or rock gardens.
Annual A plant that completes its life cycle from seed to seed in one growing season.

B

Bedding plant Any flowering plant, especially a low growing annual, planted out in large numbers in spring to provide patterns of summer color.
Biennial A plant with a two-year life cycle, being sown in one season to flower in the next.
Bolting The roped stem elongation of some plants, like cabbages, just before flowering.

C

Chlorophyll The green pigment, present in all green plants, that enables them to manufacture food materials using the energy from sunlight through photosynthesis.
Cloche A glass or plastic cover placed over outdoor plants especially at the beginning and end of the growing season to provide them with protection from cold weather.
Compost Partially decayed organic matter prepared from garden waste in a compost bin.
Cordon A method of training plants, especially fruit trees, by suppressing the growth of side branches.
Corm An underground food storage and overwintering structure produced by crocuses, gladioli and other plants.
Crown The uppermost part of a plant's roots at or close to soil level and from which the above-ground growth emerges.
Curd The edible, flowering head of a cauliflower or broccoli plant.
Cutting A part of a plant (root, stem or leaves) artificially removed and induced to form roots and develop into a new plant.

D

Dead-heading The removal of dead flower heads to stimulate new flowers to form and also prevent the development of diseases.
Deciduous Losing all leaves annually and at the same time in fall.
Dibble A blunt-ended tool used for making a hole in the soil when planting out seedlings or potatoes.
Dormant Not in active growth, a state that applies to most hardy garden plants in winter.

F

F₁ hybrid A form of hybrid plant often of exceptional vigor, large size and generally of uniform growth.
Fertilization The fusion of male and female cells following pollen transfer from a male to a female flower or flower part that results in seed and fruit development.
Forcing Forced plants are artificially brought into premature growth by giving them extra warmth in cold weather; often used for spring bulbs.
Fungicide A substance used to prevent fungal infection; some systemic fungicides can arrest fungal disease after infection has taken place.

G

Genus A group of closely related species, for example *Acer, Lilium, Rhododendron*.
Germination The emergence of a seedling from a seed.
Grafting The artificially promoted growing together and uniting of parts of two different plants.
Ground cover Low growing and widely spreading plants that have the effect of suppressing weed growth and stopping erosion.

H

Hardening-off Gradually acclimatizing plants that have been raised under protection to outdoor conditions.
Hardwood Wood from non-coniferous trees.
Hardy Able to survive outdoors all year round.
Hilling up Pulling soil around the stem base of plants to protect them from cold, a term used to describe the treatment of potato shoots early in the season.
Hybrid Of mixed parentage, usually displaying more vigor in some respect(s) than its parents.

I

Insecticide A substance, especially a chemical, used to kill insects.

L

Lime A purified form of limestone, used to render soil more alkaline.
Loam A type of soil, ideal for most garden plants, that contains a balanced blend of sand, silt, organic matter and clay.

M

Mulch A protective layer of material, especially organic matter, laid over the surface of soil to retain moisture and suppress weed growth.

N

Naturalizing Allowing plants sown or planted in a garden to seed or otherwise multiply themselves in situ.
Neutral (especially of soil), not acidic or alkaline in reaction, with a pH of about 7.
Nymph an immature stage of the life cycle of some insects.

O

Organic Strictly, a chemical containing the element carbon but usually applied to mean a pure chemical or other substance originating in or as part of some living plant or animal.

P

Perennial A plant living for more than two years, often for many years.
pH A measure of acidity and alkalinity, especially applied to garden soil and measured on a scale from 0 (very acid) to 14 (very alkaline).
Pinching Artificially removing the terminal shoot or bud to stimulate branching lower down.
Pollard The frequent cutting back of the branches of trees to the same point. This promotes the growth of more young shoots and prevents the plant from attaining its full natural size and form.
Pollination The transfer of pollen from a male to a female flower or part of a flower as a prelude to fertilization.
Potting mix A fairly sterile mixture of soil and/or peat with fertilizers, used for germinating seeds and raising and growing plants in containers.

Potting (up) Transplanting plants to larger pots to facilitate their longer term growth.

Pricking out Transplanting seedling plants into larger flats or the garden.

Propagation The artificial multiplication of plants.

Pruning The removal of parts of plants, especially in order to maintain them in a desired size and form.

R

Rootstock The roots of a plant, especially one that has had a different variety grafted onto it above ground.

Runner A shoot (such as a strawberry) that grows horizontally close to the ground and roots at intervals.

S

Seedling A young plant grown from seed, especially one before pricking out.

Self-fertile A plant or flower able to produce seeds through being fertilized with its own pollen and not requiring another individual to multiply.

Shrub A woody plant smaller than a tree, usually less than about 13 feet tall and not on a single stem.

Softwood The wood of a coniferous tree.

Species A group of individual plants or animals, alike in general features and able to interbreed readily with each other but much less readily with other groups.

Sport A plant that differs from its parents by virtue of a genetic change or malfunction having occurred.

Standard Usually applied to a flowering shrub, especially a rose, trained or grafted onto a single stem between three and six feet high.

Succulent A plant with thick and fleshy leaves and stems, usually originating from hot and dry climates.

Sucker A stem that emerges from roots at some distance from the parent plant.

T

Tender Unable to survive outdoors except in the mildest weather.

U

Undulate Wavy.

V

Variegated Of mosaic-like pattern, especially of green and yellowish leaves.

W

Widger A small, elongated spoon-like tool used for digging up seedlings.

Z

Zone A defined climatic region within a larger area and used to designate the relative hardiness of plants.

Index

Acknowledgments

The publisher thanks the following photographers and organizations for their kind permission to reproduce the photographs in this book:

1 Jerry Harpur; 2 Marijke Heuff; 3 Peter McHoy; 8–9 Georges Lévêque; 10 Heather Angel; 11 Georges Lévêque; 12 Heather Angel; 13 above Jerry Harpur (Rick Mather); 13 below Heather Angel; 14 Derek Gould; 15 Tania Midgley; 19 above Heather Angel; 19 below Stefan Buczacki; 21 left Jerry Harpur (Ken Akers); 21 right Heather Angel; 23 above Heather Angel; 23 below Harry Smith Collection; 26–27 Pictures; 28 Jerry Harpur (York Gate, Leeds); 29 above Harry Smith Collection; 29 below Tania Midgley; 30 Jerry Harpur (Beth Chatto); 31 Pamla Toler/Impact; 32 Marijke Heuff; 33 above right Michèle Lamontagne; 33 above left Tania Midgley; 33 below left Neil Holmes; 33 below right Michèle Lamontagne; 34 Jerry Harpur (John Plummer); 35 left Pat Hunt; 35 right Derek Gould; 37 Marijke Heuff; 39 above Tania Midgley; 39 centre Marijke Heuff; 39 below Tania Midgley; 40 above Pat Hunt; 40 below Jerry Harpur (Simon Hornby); 41 Derek Gould; 43 left Philippe Perdereau; 43 right Peter McHoy; 44 above Marijke Heuff (Mr & Mrs Poley-Bom); 44 below Marijke Heuff (Mien Ruys Dedems Vaart); 47 Derek Gould; 49 above Marijke Heuff; 49 below Marijke Heuff (Giardini Walda Pairon, Belgium); 51 above Stefan Buczacki; 51 below Peter McHoy; 52 left Jerry Harpur (John Plummer); 52 right Derek Gould; 54–55 Pat Hunt; 55 Derek Gould; 56 Stefan Buczacki; 57 above Jerry Harpur (Christopher Grey-Wilson); 57 below Harry Smith Collection; 58–59 Tania Midgley; 60–61 Linda Burgess; 62 Harry Smith Collection; 64 above Derek Gould; 64 centre Harry Smith Collection; 64 below Stefan Buczacki; 67 above Peter McHoy; 67 below Pat Brindley; 68 Jerry Harpur; 71 Pat Brindley; 72 above Photos Horticultural; 72 below Tania Midgley; 74–75 Heather Angel; 76–77 Tania Midgley; 77 Linda Burgess; 79 left Jacqui Hurst; 79 right Pamla Toler/Impact; 80 Marijke Heuff; 82 Eric Crichton; 83 left Jerry Harpur; 83 right Philippe Perdereau; 84 Photos Horticultural; 85 above Harry Smith Collection; 85 below Michèle Lamontagne; 86 Marijke Heuff; 87 above left Heather Angel; 87 above right Pat Brindley; 87 centre right Stefan Buczacki; 87 below Pat Brindley; 89 Eric Crichton; 90 above Pamla Toler/Impact; 90 below Tania Midgley; 92 Marijke Heuff; 93 Jerry Harpur (Mrs Dallaway, Dudley); 95 above Linda Burgess; 95 below Pamla Toler/Impact; 96 above Jerry Harpur; 96 below Jacqui Hurst; 97 Michèle Lamontagne; 98 Jacqui Hurst; 99 left Tania Midgley; 99 right Michèle Lamontagne; 100 Jacqui Hurst; 100–101 Tania Midgley; 101 above Derek Gould; 101 below Stefan Buczacki; 102 above Tania Midgley; 102 below Stefan Buczacki; 103 Harry Smith Collection; 104–105 Pat Brindley; 107 top Jerry Harpur; 107 bottom Photos Horticultural; 108 left Tania Midgley; 108 right Photos Horticultural; 109 Michèle Lamontagne; 110 Photos Horticultural; 111 Philippe Perdereau; 113 left Peter McHoy; 113 above right Peter McHoy; 113 below right Harry Smith Collection; 114 Harry Smith Collection; 115 right Jerry Harpur/Octopus Books; 115 left Photos Horticultural; 117 centre Eric Crichton; 117 above left Brian Furner Collection; 117 above right Harry Smith Collection; 117 below Harry Smith Collection; 118 above right Eric Crichton; 118 above left Harry Smith Collection; 118 below left Philippe Perdereau; 118 below right Stefan Buczacki; 120–121 Photos Horticultural; 121 left Photos Horticultural; 121 right Harry Smith Collection; 122 above Stefan Buczacki; 122 below Michèle Lamontagne; 123 Jerry Harpur; 124–125 Linda Burgess; 127 left Jerry Harpur/Octopus Books; 127 right Pat Brindley; 128 Eric Crichton; 129 Crown Copyright: Brogdale EHS; 130 above Brian Furner Collection; 130 below Peter McHoy; 131 Pat Brindley; 132 below Neil Holmes/Octopus Books; 132 above left Harry Smith Collection; 132 above right Heather Angel; 134 above and below left Harry Smith Collection; 134 below right Peter McHoy; 136 Harry Smith Collection; 137 Photos Horticultural; 139 left Tania Midgley; 139 right Marijke Heuff; 140 left Tania Midgley; 140 right Harry Smith Collection; 143 left Pat Brindley; 143 above right Pat Brindley; 143 below right Crown Copyright: Brogdale EHS; 144 above Harry Smith Collection; 144 centre Photos Horticultural; 144 below Stefan Buczacki; 146 Eric Crichton; 147 above Brian Furner Collection; 147 below Harry Smith Collection; 148 Pamla Toler/Impact; 149 Harry Smith Collection; 150–151 Michèle Lamontagne; 153 Photos Horticultural; 154 Linda Burgess; 158–159 George Wright/Octopus Books; 159 Harry Smith Collection; 160 Tania Midgley; 161 Jerry Harpur (Clive Jones); 162 left and centre Stefan Buczacki; 162 right Brian Furner Collection; 163 left Stefan Buczacki; 163 centre Harry Smith Collection; 163 right Brian Furner Collection; 164–169 Stefan Buczacki; 170–171 Philippe Perdereau; 173 Jerry Harpur (John Morley, Stoven); 174 Jacqui Hurst; 177 Marijke Heuff; 178–179 Philippe Perdereau; 180 Heather Angel.